CONTENT-AREA LITERACY:
Reaching and Teaching
THE 21ST CENTURY ADOLESCENT

HERE

MORE

Authors
Thomas Bean, Ph.D., Scott
and John Readence,
Foreword
Julie Donnelly

 SHELL EDUCATION

Publishing Credits

Dona Herweck Rice, *Editor-in-Chief*; Lee Aucoin, *Creative Director*;
Robin Erickson, *Production Director;* Timothy J. Bradley, *Illustration Manager*;
Sara Johnson, M.S.Ed., *Senior Editor*; Hillary Wolfe, *Editor*;
Juan Chavolla, *Cover and Interior Layout Designer;* Corinne Burton, M.A.Ed., *Publisher*

Shell Education

5301 Oceanus Drive
Huntington Beach, CA 92649-1030
http://www.shelleducation.com
ISBN 978-1-4258-0701-6
©2012 Shell Educational Publishing, Inc.

Table of Contents

Adolescent students are faced with far greater literacy challenges than ever before. Today's fast-paced, multi-media, digital world creates both challenges and opportunities. To support their students, educators are seeing the need to teach specific literacy skills in the content areas. *Content-Area Literacy: Reaching and Teaching the 21st Century Adolescent* provides a clear map for content-area teachers as they guide their students to mastery of their subject within today's literacy environment.

I teach social studies to adolescents and like all teachers, I must meet multiple standards while teaching students with varied learning styles. My students' ability to learn new social studies content goes hand in hand with their literacy mastery. Students who struggle to read will opt out of much learning.

Although there are many resources available to address the issue of raising literacy skills in the content area classroom, Thomas Bean, Scott Baldwin, and John Readence have put together innovative practical solutions that can be accomplished within realistic time commitments. They teach educators how to guide students to deeper comprehension by integrating literacy instruction within the content-area class. They provide methods to support differentiation. They offer engaging ideas that help *all* students ask reflective questions, acquire new vocabulary, and learn to critically analyze both print and online sources.

These talented authors have expertly designed a professional development program that brings administrators and educators together in the common goal of increasing student comprehension throughout all content areas. They make meeting the literacy challenges of the 21st century possible for both the teacher and student.

—Julie Donnelly
Author, *Guiding Adolescent Readers to Success*

INTRODUCTION

Why This Book Is Relevant

Content-Area Literacy: Reaching and Teaching the 21st Century Adolescent offers teachers an array of practical instructional strategies that target test preparation, vocabulary, comprehension, studying, critical reading, fluency, and online reading comprehension. We want to emphasize that it is crucial to think about the way in which your subject area discipline organizes knowledge and which strategies may be relevant to your particular community of practice (Moje 2008). For example, which academic vocabulary strategies will help your students develop a sense of what it means to be a biologist, a mathematician, a historian, and so on? The strategies we feature in the book are well supported by recent research syntheses (e.g., Biancarosa and Snow 2006; Lee and Spratley 2010), standards-based instruction, and content-area literacy theory and practice (e.g., Bean, Readence, and Baldwin 2012). In addition, the instructional approaches we demonstrate in the following pages are affirmed by adolescent literacy policy and position statements from major national and international professional organizations, including the National Council of Teachers of English (NCTE) and the International Reading Association (IRA), among others. While traditional print literacy remains important, we also target online digital reading processes that can be second nature for contemporary students, and yet can be one more obstacle to reading and learning for struggling readers (Bean 2010; Tapscott 2009). A new cadre of teachers, curriculum literacy leaders, and literacy coaches is taking up the challenges of literacy development in an age when the nature of text is changing and the needs of English language learners (ELL) loom. We believe that the contents of *Content-Area Literacy: Reaching and Teaching the 21st Century Adolescent* can help you and your students meet the literacy demands of learning in the 21st century.

Organization of the Book

We have organized this book to accommodate short-range and long-range staff development with a focus on a community-of-practice model that values teachers' classroom experiences and creativity in guiding students' content learning. The first section of this book describes the foundation for reading development; the next section provides a collection of research-based strategies that enhance students' performance in reading material in the content areas.

The Context for Adolescent Literacy

The first four chapters of *Content-Area Literacy: Reaching and Teaching the 21st Century Adolescent* provide a rationale for content-area reading, a brief introduction into the psychology of reading, a model for reading comprehension, and recommendations for preparing students for standardized reading tests.

Research-Based Strategies

The remainder of this book is dedicated to specific strategies for teachers of grades four through twelve that can be used to improve reading comprehension and learning across subject areas. In six chapters, we focus on strategies for vocabulary development, comprehension, study skills, critical reading, fluency, and online reading comprehension. The examples apply to subject-area content. For example, semantic mapping, a vocabulary development strategy in Chapter 5, uses the science topic *volcanoes* with a focus on disastrous volcanoes. Similarly, in Chapter 8, we use an example from economics to demonstrate the application of Opinion-Proof, a critical reading strategy for social studies.

Suggestions for Professional Development

Content-Area Literacy: Reaching and Teaching the 21st Century Adolescent is designed for both individual and collegial professional learning. Read the chapters consecutively or selectively, or start directly at the strategy section (page 76), where each strategy is presented with its own rationale and easy-to-follow directions. However, rather than offering a cookbook of reading strategies without any theory or insights into reading and learning, we feel that understanding the theory behind the strategies will assist you in selecting those which are most relevant for your students. Use this book in either a one-day in-service seminar or as a year-long professional development model, with community-of-practice seminars where teachers share their application of the strategies.

Model for Short-range Professional Development

The following guidelines will contribute to a successful professional development program:

- Limit the number of participants to no more than 30 teachers to encourage broad participation. Include principals and department chairs as well as teachers for whom teaching is a calling and not just a job.

- Maintain a high level of professionalism so that the instructional leaders who complete this in-service seminar can replicate the training or find other ways to share the strategies and disseminate the information to colleagues.

- Use a comfortable room with good acoustics and tables and chairs suitable for adults. Auditoriums, cafeterias, and classrooms typically have furniture designed for children and young adults only. A local college campus or community agency may offer an appropriate setting and can add an air of special significance. You can even conduct small professional development seminars in local restaurants that have a quiet room where teachers can meet over a meal to discuss readings and classroom application of the strategies.

- Announce the in-service seminar with enthusiasm, but do not release the book in advance. It is important that all participants work together as a group. If some of the participants have read all of the book, skimmed some of it, or simply claim to have read it, the in-service seminar may be difficult to manage.

- Inform participants that the in-service seminar will include a full day of intensive reading, writing, and brainstorming for the short-range model (see a model agenda on page 16).

- Have teachers bring one or two textbooks to the in-service seminar so that strategies for reading to learn can be discussed within an appropriate context.

- Use strategies from Chapters 5 through 9 as pre-reading, during reading, or post-reading activities to introduce Chapters 1 through 4.

- As a means of debriefing and follow-up to a short- or long-range in-service seminar, consider creating a blog (WebLog) using any one of the many blogging sites available so participants can discuss their experiences using the strategies.

- Keep the group on task and together during the program by incorporating activities such as silent reading, discussion opportunities, individual and group exercises, and self-tests. These activities can be found throughout the chapters or in the appendix. The first four chapters have logical stop points called Brain Breaks, where the facilitator can pause for group activities and ensure that participants are on the same page. As new models develop for 21st century schools, literacy leaders and teachers must work collaboratively and productively to reform education.

We look forward to joining you on this journey and supporting your efforts to provide students with engaging and powerful content-area learning and success. While we prefer the long-term professional development model for this seminar, this one-day in-service model could serve as a launching pad for longer-range work with teachers, teacher leaders, and curriculum specialists in the individual school sites. In addition, if time will not allow for an overview of the whole book, the facilitator may simply focus on the most critical needs of the group (e.g., academic vocabulary development) and related chapters.

Model Agenda for
Short-Range Professional Development

8:00–8:15	Informal introductions and coffee
8:15–8:30	Overview by the facilitator
8:30–9:00	Chapter 1: Rationale for Adolescent Literacy
9:00–9:45	Chapter 2: Learning to Read
9:45–10:00	BREAK
10:00–11:00	Chapter 3: Reading to Learn
11:00–11:45	Chapter 4: Test Preparation Strategies
11:45–12:45	LUNCH
12:45–1:00	Review of the morning and afternoon activities
1:00–1:30	Chapter 5: Strategies for Developing Vocabulary
1:30–2:00	Chapter 6: Strategies for Improving Comprehension
	Chapter 7: Strategies for Building Study Skills
2:00–2:15	BREAK
2:15–3:00	Chapter 8: Strategies for Developing Critical Reading
	Chapter 9: Strategies for Enhancing Fluency
	Chapter 10: Strategies for Enhancing Online Reading Comprehension
3:00–3:15	Wrap-up and any future debriefing and follow-up plans

Model for Long-Range Professional Development

Ultimately, we support a long-range professional development process. In working with principals and faculty in various school districts—both rural and urban—we have found that a one-year to three-year in-service seminar series dedicated to improving students' content-area literacy is most effective.

Planning for long-range professional development is more complex than planning for short-range programs. The following guidelines will help create effective professional development program:

- Engage the target group (e.g., classroom, school site, or district) of stakeholders in cooperative planning discussions to identify short- and long-range goals and steps to achieve them.

- Ensure that adequate funding is available for substitute teachers or make alternative plans to meet after school at a university site, restaurant, or other location.

- Develop a professional reading list that builds on the concepts in *Content-Area Literacy: Reaching and Teaching the 21st Century Adolescent.* Include ongoing consideration of other teaching resources related to technology integration (new literacies) and new policy and standards (e.g., Common Core Standards) that may be required.

- Use a community-of-practice model for teachers and teacher leaders. Teachers then try out the strategy and debrief at the next meeting or in a blog devoted to the project.

- Commit to at least a year-long time frame to see student progress and assess outcomes. A two- or three-year time frame is ideal, but is not always possible.

- Have an outside, external evaluation conducted to gauge the impact of the project on teachers and students.

These are general guidelines based on our own varied experiences working with classrooms, schools, and districts in small and large communities. Some of these projects have enjoyed state or district funding; others have been funded by cooperative grants in which a university and district have worked together. Still others arose from research projects with minimal funding but an ongoing interest in experimenting with progressive content-area literacy approaches. The key to the success of all of these professional development efforts is creating a community-of-practice model in which mutual respect operates to sustain both the excitement of trying new strategies and implementation over time.

Chapter Features

The chapters in this book have features designed to foster your interaction with the concepts presented within each chapter. The purpose of each feature is explained here.

- **Anticipation Guides** are designed to get you to think about and discuss the concepts presented in the chapter.

- **Targets** describe the chapter content and the relevance of that content to adolescent literacy experiences.

- **Target Vocabulary** boxes identify and define terms that are central to the chapter content.

- **Brain Breaks** and **Your Turn** activities are designed to expand on chapter content and to foster collegial conversations. These activities ensure that teachers' experiences are not overlooked in professional development sessions.

- **Suggested Self-tests** for each chapter are presented in Appendix A in three formats—matching, multiple-choice questions, and open-ended performance questions. Answers to these self-tests are provided in Appendix B.

- **Reflections on 21st Century Learning** questions at the end of each chapter help to solidify and apply the content.

Chapter 1

Rationale for Adolescent Literacy

Anticipation Guide

Place a check mark on the line indicating whether you agree or disagree with each statement.

Agree   **Disagree**

_____ _____ **1.** Every teacher should be a teacher of reading.

_____ _____ **2.** A content-area teacher's prime responsibility is to deliver subject matter information.

_____ _____ **3.** Every teacher should show students how to learn with texts.

Target

Every year, high schools in the United States churn out thousands of students who cannot read or understand the fine print on a bag of potato chips. Many more depart with reading skills so inadequate that they cannot begin to cope with today's print-based, technological culture. The public impression sees this problem as chronic and getting worse. Newspapers and politicians are eager to use American education as a scapegoat, and teachers routinely blast our public schools as they lament how much our students do not know in comparison to Japanese students today or American students of decades past.

There is also a growing realization that the United States is a multicultural society in which disenfranchised ethnic and linguistic minorities are demanding the redefinition of American schools. In addition, we are riding an immigration wave that is increasing linguistic diversity in our classrooms. Diverse and complex issues such as social equity, bilingual education, and formulas for funding public schools combine to make universal literacy one of the greatest challenges of the 21st century. For teachers and public schools, this challenge is defined by simultaneous—and sometimes conflicting—mandates and standards from the federal government, state departments of education, and accrediting bodies (Bean and Harper 2011). Our conviction is that adolescent literacy dilemmas are ultimately solvable and that each and every teacher can play a role in the resolution. Specifically, this chapter will describe some of the standard assumptions and misconceptions about adolescent literacy and investigate the common reluctance of subject-matter specialists to accept responsibility for teaching reading strategies. In addition, we will present a rationale for implementing reading strategies in the classroom with a caveat that not all strategies are relevant for every subject. Being an insider in the academic language and structure of a discipline like science or mathematics requires serious apprenticeship in the culture of the discipline. There are no generic strategies that serve as magic bullets to make this happen, but there are specific content-area teaching strategies that can help students to cope with complex texts both in print and online.

- **learning to read**—the various skills and behaviors commonly associated with the teaching of reading in the primary grades

- **reading to learn**—the process of using reading skills and strategies to learn subject-matter concepts

Assumptions and Misconceptions about Teaching Reading

Very simply put, *learning to read* concerns beginning reading (e.g., letter recognition, phonics), and *reading to learn* refers to the mental activities of more mature readers when they use reading skills to learn with texts. Learning to read is the main focus of primary school education; reading to learn is its logical extension and must be the responsibility of middle and secondary school teachers. When science and social studies teachers help students develop the strategies necessary for efficient learning from textbooks and other instructional materials, they are teachers of adolescent literacy. Unfortunately, middle and high school teachers are often reluctant to adopt an instructional emphasis that fuses reading with content. There are several reasons for this hesitancy, which include misconceptions about what it means to teach reading and false assumptions about the level of students' reading skills when they depart from elementary school.

Many teachers believe that *learning to read* and *reading to learn* are simply flip sides of the same coin. They are inclined to believe that students have—or at least should have—mastered the skills and strategies necessary to enable them to glean essential information from books and other print mediums, regardless of the format and content of the texts. They may also assume that students can—without additional instruction—integrate new information with prior knowledge and utilize textbook aids designed to refine and extend important concepts. If reading is defined in terms of elementary tasks (e.g., basic decoding skills), these assumptions are reasonable. In contrast, the assumption is pure fantasy if reading is defined in terms of subject-matter tasks (e.g., expanded homework, inquiry projects with online components, independent reading assignments, required notetaking in class, and vastly increased dependence upon multiple textbooks with varied and complex organizational patterns and graphics). It is not true that students will automatically modify elementary reading skills to suit subject-matter reading demands. In order to get a feeling for the demands of complex text, try the following activity.

Activity: Check Your Comprehension

Read the following paragraph and summarize it in your own words from recall.

We are completely in agreement with him on this point: That symbolization is constitutive of symbolic consciousness will trouble no one who believes in the absolute value of the Cartesian cogito. But it must be understood that if symbolization is constitutive of consciousness, it is permissible to perceive that there is an immanent bond of comprehension between the symbolization and the symbol (Sartre 1948).

Did you have difficulty comprehending the passage? If you were familiar with existential philosophy, you may have breezed right through it. However, if this material was foreign to your own personal experiences, your reading comprehension was probably pretty poor. In order to read this passage with full understanding, you would have to acquire some very specialized background knowledge and new academic vocabulary in the field of philosophy. Which aspects of the paragraph and your background knowledge most affected your comprehension?

The textbooks you use every semester may seem just as murky to the students in your classes. Students lack experiential background and are unfamiliar with the vocabulary and sophisticated concepts found in social studies, science, and other subject areas. It is presumptuous, and possibly damaging, to expect students to perform well automatically with subject-matter texts. Many students struggle with their textbooks because they are overwhelmed by the scope and complexity of the material and because they have never been taught relevant content-area reading strategies. Many teachers and students can benefit from the growing array of literacy strategies available for assisting students in reading and learning with print and digital texts.

Brain Break

Curiosity and Clarification

Generate one curiosity or clarification question regarding the misconceptions about teaching reading. Discuss your statement with other teachers.

Reexamining the Roles of Teachers and Texts

When subject-matter teachers are surveyed concerning their attitude toward teaching reading in the content areas, they typically grimace at the saying, "Every teacher is a teacher of reading." Ask this same set of teachers their opinion about the statement, "every teacher should show students how to learn with texts in their disciplines," and you will hear a more favorable response. Because the second statement connotes a model of reading instruction that focuses on content knowledge rather than isolated reading skills, subject-matter teachers recognize its relevance to their teaching. In the past, reading in secondary schools has been associated with isolated, remedial skills instruction when, in fact, the emphasis should be on reading strategies that enhance learning in science, mathematics, and other subject areas.

We agree with this reemphasis. Content teachers should be catalysts for learning, and their responsibility is to aid students in reading and learning with text. The focus of content-reading instruction is on *reading to learn*, not on learning to read. Let us examine in-depth the roles of the teacher, the reader, and the textbook as each relates to success in learning. First, if texts were meant to be read in isolation, there would be little, if any, need for someone called a teacher. Similarly, if texts were so easy to read that a reader needed little or no help to learn the material, a teacher, again, would be superfluous. Yet, as the Sartre philosophy passage illustrates, this is not normally the case with text materials. Texts are usually difficult for adolescent readers who need specific reading strategies in order to master the content of subject-area textbooks. Furthermore, it makes sense to describe content reading as a means of improving communication. There is a sort of long-distance communication that should develop between an author of a text and a reader. The reader should, in effect, attempt to communicate with authors of texts by constructing meaning from their words and thoughts. Given the goal of the reader and the difficulty of texts, as facilitators, teachers need to promote the interaction between readers and texts. The teacher's role in adolescent literacy is to encourage the thinking processes essential to understanding and learning with print and online texts. Teachers can promote this valuable interaction if they think of themselves as facilitators of the learning process. In addition, teachers have inherent advantages over textbooks, computers, the Internet, or any other teaching tools because good teachers know how to:

- **Tailor the message** by adapting their presentations to the needs, abilities, and experiential backgrounds of their students. Teachers already know what their students know and what they do not know, and can interact with them during their presentations.

- **Activate prior knowledge** by reminding students of what they know and how it relates to what they are learning.

- **Focus attention** by increasing students' interest and motivation to learn new material and by directing them to pay attention to selected pieces of the text.

- **Monitor comprehension** by checking to see if students understand important parts of a text presentation. Teachers, not materials, do the teaching, and this teaching includes helping students acquire the strategies essential to learning with texts.

Brain Break

Curiosity and Clarification

Generate one curiosity or clarification question about the role of teachers in introducing students to text. Discuss your statement with other teachers.

Summary

This chapter provided a rationale for specific content-area reading strategies. The assumptions and misconceptions presently surrounding content-area reading have been listed and discussed. Adolescent literacy has been offered as a viable means by which to emphasize learning with text.

Reflections on 21st Century Learning

1. List the pros and cons of both a short-range and a long-range professional development program for your site. Which plan is best suited to your situation?

2. How will you get key players to participate in professional development?

3. What does reading to learn mean to you? How are you helping students access the content in the texts for your specific subject area?

Learning To Read

Anticipation Guide

Place a check mark on the line indicating whether you agree or disagree with each statement.

Agree   Disagree

_____   _____   **1.** In adult reading, the eyes move smoothly from left to right.

_____   _____   **2.** Learning to read is mostly about "busting the code."

_____   _____   **3.** There are four sounds in the word *father*.

Target

Chapter 2 focuses on learning to read—the various skills and behaviors commonly associated with the teaching of reading in the primary grades. Our purpose in presenting this information is to give you a basic understanding of the mental processes involved in beginning reading. For students, understanding the reading process is essential to the successful implementation and adaptation of content-area reading strategies. It is good to know how to do something, but it is even better to know why we do something.

Some children begin kindergarten with well-developed reading skills. Others begin school without the ability to name a single letter of the alphabet. In any case, our societal expectation is that all children will learn to read in elementary school regardless of English language proficiency, intellectual ability, or home environment. It would be difficult to overstate the challenge to our colleagues in the primary grades. This chapter should give you an appreciation for the complexity of the skills children must master before they are capable of applying the research-based reading strategies presented later in the book.

The burden of new vocabulary in this chapter is very high, but the terminology is essential to comprehending the chapter and communicating with colleagues about the processes involved in learning to read. Each of the terms listed on page 31 is introduced in this chapter and defined in a proper context. In order to prepare your mind to receive new information, read each new word or phrase three times in rapid succession—aloud if you are alone. Then read the definition once. This procedure will take two or three minutes, but you will find that the chapter seems easier to read and you will have better comprehension. (Your instructor or in-service coordinator may model one of the strategies from Chapter 5: Strategies for Developing Vocabulary, as an objective lesson in teaching and learning new words.)

TARGET VOCABULARY

- **decoding**—the conversion of written text to spoken language equivalents

- **fixation**—the window of information when the eyes are at rest on a line of print

- **fluency**—fast, accurate, and effortless decoding

- **fonts**—the various styles of printed and written letters

- **letter recognition**—the ability to distinguish one letter from another

- **ligatures**—the lines and strokes that connect written letters

- **phonemic awareness**—the ability to distinguish one speech sound from another

- **phonics**—a set of rules for associating sounds with letters

- **pursuit eye movements**—the action of the eyes when following a moving target

- **regressions**—the action of the eyes when moving backwards on a line of print

- **return sweeps**—the action of the eyes moving from the end of one line of print to the beginning of the next

- **saccadic (sa-KAD-ik) eye movements**—the action of the eyes when moving from one fixed object to another

- **sight vocabulary**—written words that are recognized instantly and without effort

- **word recognition**—the ability to see a written word and recite it

The Reading Process

Remember the first time you had to assemble a swing set, a crib, or a picnic table using those convenient multilingual directions that came with the product? You probably discovered more evidence to support one of Murphy's Laws: Almost everything is simple— once you know how to do it. The same is true for reading. It is easy for us as literate adults, having mastered the act of reading, to underestimate the complexity of the task. In order to illustrate the point, we will provide a brief introduction to eye movements in reading. (It will be useful to have a partner as you work through the rest of the chapter.)

Eye Movements

There are two types of eye movements in human beings: pursuit movement and saccadic movement. *Pursuit eye movements* are used to follow a moving target such as an ice skater moving across the rink or a ball flying through the air. To observe pursuit eye movement, hold a finger in the air and ask your partner to follow it as you move it around. You will see your partner's eyes move smoothly from side to side and up and down with the movement of your finger. *Saccadic eye movements* are not at all smooth; they are quick little jumps the eyes make when moving from one stationary target to another. To see saccades, ask your partner to look from object to object in the room while you watch his or her eyes. Reading is accomplished with saccadic eye movements because the words on a page are stationary, making it impossible to read with pursuit eye movements.

Activity: Observing Saccadic Eye Movements

YOUR TURN

To convince yourself that reading is accomplished with saccadic eye movements, place your finger or a pencil under the beginning of a line of print in this book.

Focus your eyes on the tip of your finger and then move your finger across the page without allowing your eyes to stop. If you do this properly, the words will appear only as a blur. In order to see letters and words with sufficient clarity for reading, the eyes must be stationary on the line of print.

In addition to saccades, three visual activities occur during reading: fixations, regressions, and return sweeps. *Fixations* occur between saccades. During a fixation, the eyes are at rest on the line of print, allowing the reader to see a window of letters and words clearly. The number of letters and words seen in each fixation varies from individual to individual, depends upon the difficulty of the text, and averages only 10–12 letter spaces for most adults, about two words. Readers also make backward saccades in order to confirm a thought or capture information missed from a previous fixation. These backward saccades are called *regressions*.

The final type of eye movement involved in reading is called the *return sweep*. This is the journey the eyes make when moving from the end of one line of print to the beginning of the next. Normal adult reading proceeds as a sequence of saccades, fixations, regressions, and return sweeps. Saccades, regressions, and return sweeps are so fast (about one-fiftieth of a second) that most readers are unaware of them. A fixation can be as long as two seconds for beginning readers and as brief as one-fifth of a second in adults.

Learning to control the eyes during reading and developing efficient visual search procedures are never part of the elementary school curriculum. In effect, children must teach themselves through practice, and beginners expend considerable mental energy on these tasks. As an adult fluent reader, your mind makes all the calculations necessary to direct the eyes without any conscious attention on your part.

Activity: Peephole Experiment

Take a blank piece of paper and fold it in half lengthwise. Fold it in half again width-wise. Then, tear off the corner where the two folds meet. When you unfold the paper you should have a hole about the size of a quarter in the middle of the paper. At the top of the paper write two sentences describing your favorite vacation spot or your in-laws' most irritating habits. Finally, hold the paper up with the sentences facing out for your partner to read while you look through the hole at your partner's eyes. You should have no difficulty observing saccades, fixations, regressions, and return sweeps.

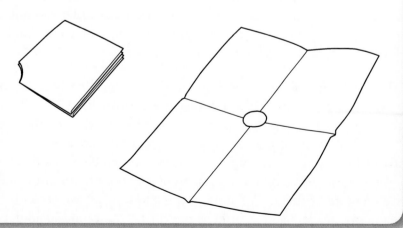

Brain Break

Curiosity and Clarification

Generate one curiosity or clarification question about eye movements and reading. Discuss your statement with other teachers.

Behind the Eyes

The visual information from each fixation is stored in temporary memory while the mind recognizes and organizes the letters and words, puts them together into phrases and sentences, interprets their meanings, and then integrates the new information with the reader's existing knowledge. For children learning to read, state standards focus primarily on skills related to word recognition and, to a lesser extent, on reading comprehension.

Decoding

The skills associated with learning to read are reflected in the K–3 standards of every state. The most important standard is the development of *decoding*, the ability to convert written text into language equivalents. *Fluency* refers to the ability to decode words rapidly and automatically and to put those words together in natural sounding phrases and sentences. In order to become fluent, children must learn to recognize and distinguish the individual sounds of spoken language and the letters that make up written words. The ability to do this is commonly referred to as *phonemic awareness*—having the ability to distinguish the individual speech sounds of a language known as *phonemes*. This is not as easy as it may appear. If you ask the average kindergartner how many sounds there are in *dog*, the most likely response, assuming that the child can count, will be "one." Recognizing and pronouncing individual speech sounds is not a natural human behavior because most language sounds do not occur in isolation, but only in conjunction with other sounds. For example, the sound we usually associate with the letter *k* is never produced in isolation in natural speech; it is always attached to other sounds. Note that when you say the name of the letter *k* you have attached a vowel sound to it (e.g., /*kay*/). It can take children months or even years to learn how to recognize and distinguish the individual sounds of English with facility. The task is even more daunting for children whose first language is not English.

Letter Recognition

Children must also master *letter recognition,* the ability to identify the letters of the alphabet and to distinguish one from the other. This also is not a simple task for five- and six-year-old minds because they must learn to instantly recognize the upper and lower case letters in all of their manifestations. There are hundreds of different fonts in written English, and fluent reading requires the ability to recognize the distinctive characteristics of each letter in spite of striking variations in letter shape, size, and spacing. Children who are learning to read words with Times New Roman (font #1 in figure 2.1) might have difficulty with words written in Ariel Narrow (font #2 in figure 2.1); and Free Style Script (font #5 in figure 2.1) would be very difficult because the letter shapes are different from Times New Roman and because of the additional lines—called *ligatures*—connecting the letters.

Fig. 2.1 Examples of Fonts

Examples of Fonts

1. Father

2. Father

3. **Father**

4. *Father*

5. *Father*

Phonics and Word Recognition

While children are learning phonemic awareness and letter recognition skills, they are typically also learning phonics: a system of rules that allows the reader to assign language sounds to individual letters (e.g., *s* or *d*), groups of letters (e.g., *sh* or *ing*), or different sounds to the same letter or combination of letters based upon the context in which the letters occur (e.g., the letter *a* in *mad* and *made*). Phonics rules are really generalizations with huge numbers of circumstances in which they do not work (e.g., the silent *k* in *knight* or the *o* in *women* that sounds like the *i* in *fit*).

In the parlance of beginning reading instruction, the pronunciation of individual words is referred to as *word recognition*—seeing a written word and speaking or thinking its oral language equivalent. Phonics, a valuable tool in learning to read, can only provide clues for word recognition. In addition, analyzing each word every time it is encountered would be highly inefficient. Therefore, in order to become fluent readers, children must develop a *sight vocabulary*: words that the reader can pronounce instantly without mentally breaking them down into individual letters and applying phonics rules. Any word which is read for the first time—by a reader at any age—will first be broken down into smaller parts and then pronounced. For example, if you have never read the word *exculpate* before, you were just now forced to break down the word into its component letters and then apply phonics rules in an attempt to pronounce it. Repetitive readings of words eventually result in written words becoming sight words. A good sight vocabulary for first-grade students is several hundred words. A high school student with good word recognition skills should have a sight vocabulary in excess of 20,000 words.

State standards for K–3 reading focus on phonemic awareness, letter recognition, phonics, word recognition, development of sight vocabulary, and reading fluency. Taken as a group, these standards are all directly related to decoding. Most states also have standards related to reading comprehension, vocabulary development (learning new word meanings), and reference skills. However, the truth is that learning to read is mostly about busting the code, and that is what most distinguishes learning to read from reading to learn.

Curiosity and Clarification

Generate one curiosity or clarification question about decoding. Discuss your statement with other teachers.

Summary

The reading process is a complex set of mental activities that include K–12 curriculum standards such as letter and word recognition, as well as self-taught skills such as control of eye movements. Most states have standards for reading comprehension, vocabulary development, and other aspects of literacy unrelated to decoding. However, learning to convert text into an oral language equivalent is the fundamental challenge of learning to read.

Reflections on 21st Century Learning

1. How can you determine your students' abilities to decode?

2. Examine your current lessons and assignments. Are there simple ways you can adjust your current lessons to assist students who may have difficulty decoding (e.g., change the fonts of your assignments)?

Chapter 3

Reading To Learn

Anticipation Guide

Place a check mark on the line indicating whether you agree or disagree with each statement.

Agree   Disagree

_____ _____ **1.** Human beings can attend to two activities at the same time.

_____ _____ **2.** Comprehension is impossible without prior knowledge of the topic.

_____ _____ **3.** The ability to daydream while reading is a good thing.

Target

Comprehension of challenging ideas in a content area is rarely easy for students, and no collection of textbook aids can be a substitute for the careful guidance you can provide. In order to accomplish this in your particular content area, you should have a working knowledge of the comprehension process and an array of strategies at your disposal. In this chapter, we will introduce a model of the reading process. This model will illustrate the major psychological processes that support reading comprehension and learning.

Each of the terms listed on the following page is introduced in this chapter and defined in a proper context. In order to prepare your mind to receive new information, read each target word or phrase three times in rapid succession—aloud if you are alone. Then read the definition once. This procedure will take a minute or so, but you will find that the chapter seems easier to read, and you will have better comprehension.

TARGET VOCABULARY

- **attention**—the focused application of the mind on an object or thought

- **automaticity**—the ability to engage in multiple tasks simultaneously because all but one of them can be accomplished without conscious attention

- **conscious attention**—the layman's notion of paying attention as opposed to daydreaming

- **experience-based questions**—questions with answers that cannot be derived from the text

- **learning**—the expansion of an individual's store of knowledge to include new concepts and vocabulary

- **metacognition**—awareness of one's own mental processes

- **prior knowledge**—the complete storage of an individual's experiences, memories, vocabulary, and concepts

- **reading to learn**—the process of using reading to acquire content-area concepts

- **scripts**—a person's knowledge of procedures, routines, and activities

- **selective attention**—the ability to screen out irrelevant information while focusing on one thing

- **text-explicit questions**—questions for which the answers are directly stated in the text

- **text-implicit questions**—questions for which the answers must be inferred from the text

- **topic interest**—the reader's natural enthusiasm for the subject matter of a given text

The Role of Attention in Reading

Attention can be defined as a focusing of consciousness or the application of the mind on a particular object or thought. Attention is the engine that powers the reading machine. The more attention readers generate during reading, the better their comprehension and learning will be. One type of attention is *conscious attention*, the common sense variety most often defined in such expressions as "stop daydreaming and pay attention." A second type of attention is *selective attention*, which refers to the ability to screen out unwanted information and to focus on one particular mental task. For example, imagine that you are at a crowded party with dozens of conversations going on around you. One group is complaining about the football team, another conversation is about a wedding, yet another is an animated discussion about the stock market, and so on. You are capable of listening and attending to any of these conversations while screening out the others; and then, without even moving your head, you are capable of switching your attention to a different conversation and tuning in to it while tuning out the others.

Automaticity

It is also interesting to note that human beings are capable of giving conscious attention to only one task at a time. If you are engaged in more than one task at the same time, all but one of them must be done automatically. It is, of course, possible to switch rapidly back and forth, but the mind can only attend consciously to one task at a time. Remember your first driving experience? You were steering the car, but when it came time to apply the brake you found yourself drifting to the left or right because you stopped steering. Signaling, braking, accelerating, shifting, steering, and applying your makeup or shaving (just kidding) were all things that required your conscious attention. Now you can drive home from work without paying any conscious attention to the mechanics of driving. You are able to think of other things while you drive because the mechanics of driving have been automated. If you had to think about steering, braking, and applying the gas, you would have little attention left to think about things unrelated to driving. In a sense, you are capable of setting yourself on automatic pilot when you drive, thus freeing your conscious attention for other mental activities. The ability of the human mind to regulate itself in this fashion is referred to as *automaticity*, a mental process absolutely essential in reading to learn.

Reading Model: Stage 1

You have probably had the following experience hundreds of times. You are reading a book and suddenly realize that your conscious attention has wandered. Instead of concentrating on the text, you have been thinking about a past personal triumph or how to weasel out of some future commitment you made in a moment of weakness. Suddenly, you snap back to the task at hand and realize you have comprehended nothing in spite of the fact that your eyes have been moving dutifully from left to right and your inner voice has been repeating words in your mind. You were on autopilot for reading. You were decoding and you were fluent, but there was no comprehension of the text. The model of the reading process pictured in Figure 3.1 represents a daydreaming adult on autopilot or a student whose own internal definition of reading is nothing more than decoding print to sound without attention to comprehension. Paradoxically, the ability to daydream while reading is essential for reading to learn because when no attention is required for decoding and fluency, the reader's conscious attention can be fully devoted to the meaning of the text.

Description of the Model

The reader utilizes the lowest possible level of attention in reading. The reader's autopilot decodes the words into spoken language equivalents and mechanically puts them together in phrases and sentences with proper intonation. However, because conscious attention is focused elsewhere, there is little or no comprehension. Figure 3.1 displays Reading Model: Stage 1.

Fig. 3.1. Reading Model: Stage 1

```
┌─────────────────────────┐          ┌─────────────────────────┐
│       ATTENTION          │          │    Cognitive Focus       │
│   ┌─────────────────┐    │ ───────▶ │   ┌─────────────────┐   │
│   │     Level 1     │    │          │   │    Autopilot    │   │
│   └─────────────────┘    │          │   └─────────────────┘   │
└─────────────────────────┘          └─────────────────────────┘
                                                  │
                                                  ▼
                                     ┌─────────────────────────┐
                                     │    Reading Ability       │
                                     │       Achieved:          │
                                     │   ┌─────────────────┐   │
                                     │   │    Decoding     │   │
                                     │   └─────────────────┘   │
                                     │           │             │
                                     │           ▼             │
                                     │   ┌─────────────────┐   │
                                     │   │    Fluency      │   │
                                     │   └─────────────────┘   │
                                     │                         │
                                     │   ┌─────────────────┐   │
                                     │   │  Comprehension  │   │
                                     │   └─────────────────┘   │
                                     └─────────────────────────┘
```

Instructional Implications

This stage of reading has two implications for instruction. First, a good autopilot is essential for reading to learn. Students who have not acquired basic decoding skills should be referred to a reading specialist. The strategies for enhancing fluency in chapter 9 may be useful for such students. Second, students who appear to have adequate decoding skills and an autopilot must understand that reading is much more than just saying the words. They must learn to think at the same time they are reading the text. Encourage students to think while reading. The strategies in Chapter 6 are designed to encourage thinking during reading.

Brain Break

Curiosity and Clarification

Generate one curiosity or clarification question about attention.
Discuss your statement with other teachers.

Prior Knowledge and Comprehension

How many times in your teaching career have you answered a student's question by beginning with the phrase, "It's sort of like..."? The necessity of explaining new concepts to students by relating it to their prior knowledge—what they already know and understand—is a fundamental strategy of the teaching profession. This strategy is often referred to as "relating the new to the known." Fortunately, teachers can exert some degree of control over this aspect of comprehension. Through guided instruction, teachers can activate, appraise, and, if need be, increase students' knowledge of a topic before they begin learning with the text.

Prior knowledge is composed of memories, vocabulary (word meanings), and *scripts* (knowledge of procedures, routines, and activities). A student's prior knowledge is a critical factor in comprehending new information from reading. If the student's prior knowledge is equal to the information in the text, there is nothing to be learned because the information is redundant. On the other hand, if the students have too little prior knowledge, reading comprehension will be difficult or impossible because the students will be unable to relate the new to the known.

Activity: Prior Knowledge and Comprehension

Read the following sentence and see if you can figure out what it means: *The Phos-chek™ dropped left of the Cat™.*

If you lived in a canyon area in Southern California where the early autumn Santa Ana winds spread wild fires that regularly destroy homes and forests, the term *Phos-chek™* would be very familiar from numerous news reports and personal experience. In firefighting operations, *Phos-chek™*, a fire retardant, is dropped from helicopters. The term *Cat™* refers to a Caterpillar™ tractor cutting a fire line near where the chemical fire retardant is being dropped.

Reading Model: Stage 2

Knowing the meanings of *Phos-chek™* and *Cat™* are critical to the comprehension of the sentence, but comprehension will be superficial unless the reader is also familiar with firefighting. If, in addition, the reader has memories of Southern California fires—either from direct personal experience or from the media—reading comprehension will be even better. Stage 2 of our reading model illustrates the importance of prior knowledge in reading.

Description of the Model

In Stage 2, the autopilot is working, but the reader's conscious attention is focused on comprehending the text. The reader relates the new information in the text with his or her prior knowledge, and there is some expansion of prior knowledge. However, learning tends to be accidental rather than purposeful. Stage 2 reading characterizes the majority of middle and high school students and is inadequate for meeting the proficiency demands of 21st century reading. Figure 3.2 displays Reading Model: Stage 2.

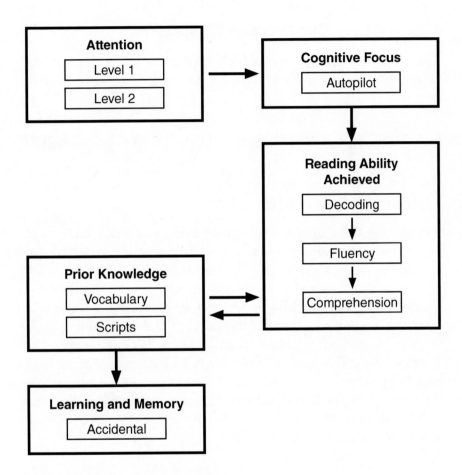

Fig. 3.2. Reading Model: Stage 2

Instructional Implications

Anything teachers can do to amplify or activate students' prior knowledge of the subject area before reading will increase reading comprehension. Introducing and reinforcing vocabulary and providing students with relevant background knowledge are essential, especially with challenging texts. Chapter 5 provides strategies for vocabulary development.

Brain Break

Curiosity and Clarification

Generate one curiosity or clarification question about the role of prior knowledge in reading. Discuss your statement with other teachers.

Reading to Learn with Text

Learning is the expansion and restructuring of prior knowledge to include new concepts and vocabulary as well as to correct preexisting misconceptions. Unfortunately, it is possible for readers to comprehend text without learning anything. Students frequently understand the words and sentences on a superficial level as they progress through the text, but end up retaining little. This is most often the case when students are indifferent to or bored with the material, or if the text is difficult and so dense with new information that students are unable to determine what is and what is not important. Students who are capable of reading and comprehending, but choose not to, are frequently referred to as apathetic or unmotivated readers.

Motivation

In the context of reading to learn, motivation refers to the reader's desire to focus attention and mental energy on comprehension and learning. Motivation may be influenced by external incentives such as grades or teacher approval or disapproval. It may also be affected by internal drives such as the need to acquire specific information or the self-satisfaction that comes from learning. High levels of reader motivation—regardless of source—will result in high levels of attention to comprehension and learning.

Topic Interest

Topic interest refers to the reader's natural enthusiasm for the subject matter of a given text. One way to increase students' attention and learning during reading is to give them texts that are of interest to them. There is a strong relationship between reading interest and comprehension. Content teachers are not likely to be in a position to arrange a curriculum that has universal appeal to juveniles and adolescents. However, it is possible to engage most students in prereading activities that will stimulate interest in expository reading assignments. Text Appetizers, Polar Opposites, Phony Documents, and other strategies from Chapters 6 and 8 are designed to build enthusiasm and interest for reading assignments.

Purpose

It is sometimes true that students are highly motivated to read and learn, but are unable to do so because they do not know how or where to focus their attention during reading. In the beginning stages of learning to read, children tend to adopt a memorization strategy for answering the comprehension questions that follow oral and silent reading sessions. Texts are short in the primary grades, so teacher questioning tends to cover all of the facts and statements in the text. For example:

- "What was the name of the girl in the story?"

- "What was the name of the boy?"

- "What was the name of the dog?"

- "Where were the children going?"

- "Why did they take the dog with them?"

- "How big was the dog?"

Under these conditions, memorizing the events and facts of the story is an effective strategy. However, as children progress to the middle grades and begin encountering longer and more complex expository texts, this memorization strategy will betray them. Because they find it impossible to commit the content of the text to memory, many students eventually drift onto autopilot without any serious attempt to comprehend or learn. Their purpose in reading may be little more than getting to the end of the reading assignment. It is critical that teachers establish purposes for reading so that students' attention is clearly focused on what is important in the reading assignment.

Metacognition

Metacognition refers to awareness of one's own mental processes; that is, it entails an effort to manage your own thoughts through conscious planning. People who have good metacognitive skills understand their own behaviors, employ mental strategies that they can verbalize, and evaluate the quality of their thinking. On the other hand, young people frequently do not understand or even attempt to monitor their own thought processes. Many rove mindlessly through a textbook assignment without any clearly defined purposes or conscious strategies for learning. Current research in the area of metacognition indicates that students who have good metacognitive skills are better comprehenders (Baker and Beall 2009; Cartwright 2009). Therefore, helping your students develop their metacognitive awareness is fundamental to teaching study strategies.

Reading Model: Stage 3

If you have ever generated a question that you hope will be answered by the text you are about to read, you have used Reading Model: Stage 3.

Description of the Model

In Stage 3, the autopilot is working: the reader's conscious attention is at a very high level and focused on comprehending the text, the reader relates the new information in the text with his or her prior knowledge, and there is a significant expansion and restructuring of prior knowledge. The reader is metacognitively alert. Learning and recall of information are purposeful rather than accidental. Stage 3, illustrated in figure 3.3, is a model of proficient reading and defines what students must be able to do in order to meet the reading demands of a 21st century global workforce.

Fig. 3.3. Reading Model: Stage 3

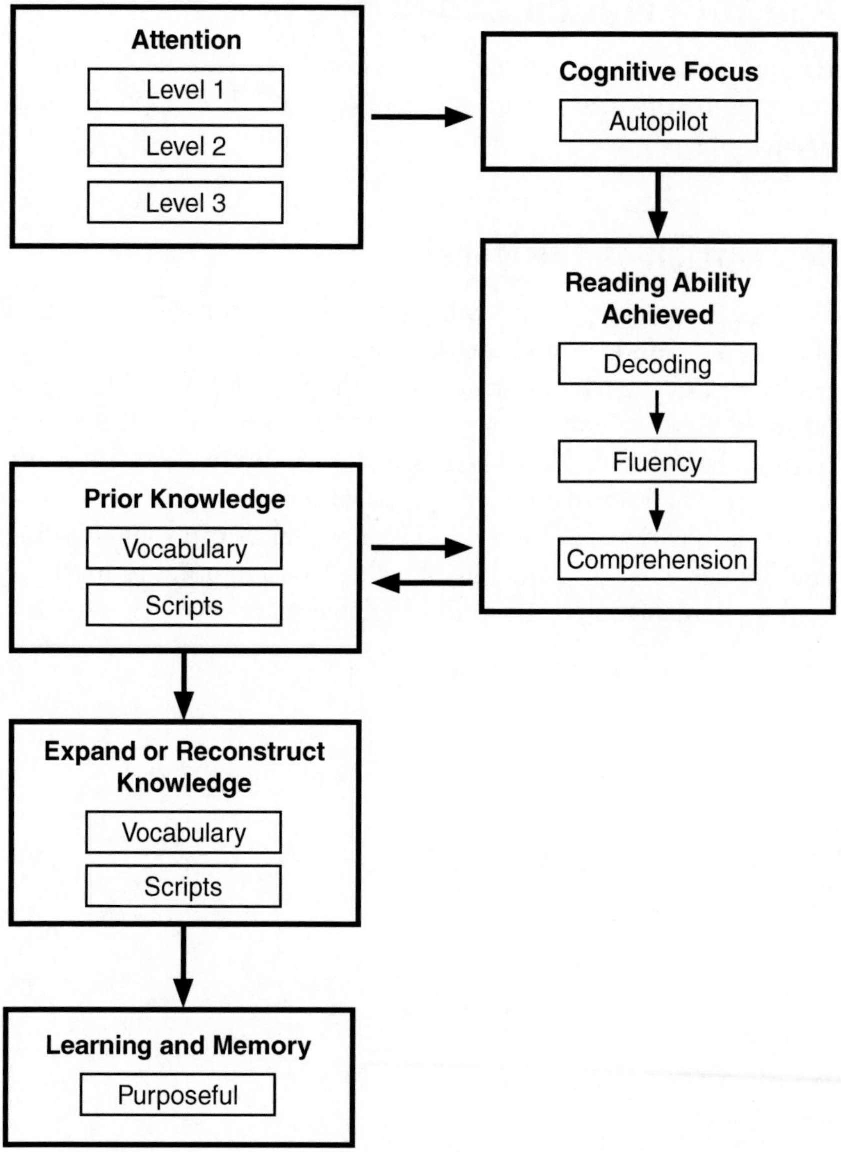

Attention
- Level 1
- Level 2
- Level 3

Cognitive Focus
- Autopilot

Reading Ability Achieved
- Decoding
- Fluency
- Comprehension

Prior Knowledge
- Vocabulary
- Scripts

Expand or Reconstruct Knowledge
- Vocabulary
- Scripts

Learning and Memory
- Purposeful

Instructional Implications

Anything teachers can do to increase topic interest and establish clear purposes for reading will also increase attention and focus on comprehension, learning, and the retention of important subject-area knowledge. Chapters 6, 7, and 8 offer a variety of strategies for improving comprehension, retention, and critical thinking.

Brain Break

Curiosity and Clarification

Generate one curiosity or clarification question about reading to learn with text. Discuss your statement with other teachers.

Levels of Comprehension and Questioning

Locating answers to questions hinges, in part, on knowing how comprehension questions are structured. Some questions simply require a low level matching strategy. For example, the question asks, "What color was the salesman's hair in the story?" and the text in the story states, "The salesman had steel gray hair." A simple matching of the question to the information in the story is a start to comprehension. Comprehension questions always signal where the information may be found—sometimes right in the text, other times through knowledge the reader has that must be marshaled when the text only supplies hints that require educated guesses and inferencing.

Levels of Comprehension

Comprehension and mastery of content material frequently demand in-depth study beyond the factual, literal level. A content teacher can guide this process during the reading stage by ensuring that students adopt an active, questioning approach to the text based on their prior knowledge and experiences. In order to construct lessons that guide students in the assimilation of text concepts with their own experiences, it is helpful to have a procedure for characterizing different levels of comprehension and types of questions. These categories are *text explicit, text implicit,* and *experience-based.* This simple framework captures the essence of comprehension—the interaction of prior experience with printed information.

Activity: Understanding Categories of Comprehension and Questioning

YOUR TURN

In order to gain a more concrete understanding of the three categories, read the paragraph and answer the questions that follow.

> Forgetfulness is a problem that plagues most of us. We forget to perform routine tasks like stopping at the grocery store on the way home or picking up the dry-cleaning. Worse still, we may forget important things such as a new student's name, the mortgage payment, or our spouse's birthday. Fortunately, there are solutions to our forgetfulness.

1. Based on the paragraph above, what problem plagues most of us?

2. What specific group or audience is the paragraph addressing?

3. What is your solution(s) to the problem posed in the paragraph?

The answer to question 1—*forgetfulness*—is *text explicit* because the answer can be extracted directly from the text. You can point to the answer in the paragraph. Typically, *text explicit* questions have only one correct answer. For discussions with students, *on the page* is a good alternative name for *text explicit*.

The answer to question 2—*teachers*—is *text implicit* because the correct response does not come directly from the text; you cannot point to the answer in the paragraph. Rather, it has to be inferred from hints in the passage, a strategy that is often referred to as *reading between the lines*. The phrase, *a new student's name*, suggests that the audience consists of either students or teachers. However, the activities cited in the paragraph are adult activities, which rule out students as the intended audience. Text implicit questions usually have only one correct answer, but sometimes there are several. For discussions with students, *think-and-search* is a good alternative name for text implicit.

There is no correct answer to question 3 because it requires a response based on personal knowledge. *Experience-based* answers are derived from one's previous experience and not the text itself. In this case, you had to search your prior knowledge for strategies that combat forgetfulness. Experience-based questions usually have many possible answers, and there are no right or wrong answers, although some answers may be better than others. A good answer does not come directly from the text. The reader cannot point to the answer in the text, nor is it possible to infer the solution based on a set of clues. Experience-based comprehension is at the heart of critical reading, invention, and problem solving, and it is a frequently neglected form of questioning in middle and secondary classrooms. For discussions with students, *on your own* is a good alternative name for experience-based. The distinctions among the three levels are summarized in figure 3.4.

Fig. 3.4. Levels of Comprehension

Levels	Information Source			# of Possible Answers	Alternate Definitions
	Question	Inference	Answer		
Text explicit	text	no	text	one	on the page
Text implicit	text	yes	text	one plus	think-and-search
Experience-based	text	yes	reader	many	on your own

Questioning

Questions are the most common means of comprehension instruction. Questions are used to activate students' prior knowledge, establish purposes for reading, generate interest in the topic, focus attention on significant aspects of text material, and aid students in reading beyond the literal, text explicit level. Teachers who ask good questions promote the processes of comprehension and learning. Chapters 6, 7, and 8 include numerous question-based strategies for improving reading comprehension, study skills, and critical reading.

Brain Break

Curiosity and Clarification

Generate one curiosity or clarification question about levels of understanding. Discuss your statement with other teachers.

Summary

A model of the reading process was introduced in stages in order to explain the relationships among attention, prior knowledge, and learning and to illustrate how reading comprehension and learning can be improved by enhancing the reader's attention, interest, motivation, and prior knowledge. This chapter also presented a three-tiered model of levels of comprehension and questioning.

Reflections on 21t Century Learning

1. How can you assess your students' prior knowledge?

2. What are some ways you can increase student motivation and generate more interest in your topic?

Chapter 4

Test Preparation Strategies

Anticipation Guide

Place a check mark on the line indicating whether you agree or disagree with each statement.

Agree   **Disagree**

_____   _____   **1.** Most state reading assessments are valid tests.

_____   _____   **2.** Prepping students for reading tests is a waste of time.

_____   _____   **3.** Writing should be a part of state reading assessments.

Target

The reading achievement test used in your state is not an isolated phenomenon. It is part of a nationwide pattern of high stakes testing and public school accountability being driven by No Child Left Behind (Conley and Hinchman 2004). Understanding the nature of state reading assessments is essential in assisting students in achieving higher scores without sacrificing curriculum standards in your subject area.

Each of the terms listed on the next page is introduced in this chapter and defined in a proper context. In order to prepare your mind to receive new information, read each target word or phrase three times in rapid succession—aloud if you are alone. Then read the definition once. This procedure will take a minute or so, but you will find that the chapter seems easier to read, and you will have better comprehension.

TARGET VOCABULARY

- **mirror assessment**—classroom assessments that reflect the format of a standardized test

- **mirror assessment strategy**—a set of guidelines for designing classroom tests that reflects the format of your state reading assessment for middle and secondary students

- **passage dependent items**—test questions that cannot be answered without reading the passages to which they refer

- **passage independent items**—test questions that can be answered without reading the passages to which they refer

- **performance items**—test questions that require written responses from students

- **test validity**—the extent to which a test measures what it claims to measure

- **testwiseness**—a series of principles that can be applied to exams independently of subject-area knowledge

National Overview of State Reading Assessments

Only a few years ago, the United States federal government enacted No Child Left Behind (2001) which mandated yearly state assessments of reading in grades 3 through 8. This mandate has promoted a high-stakes testing environment in which teachers and students spend huge amounts of time on test preparation at the expense of music, art, health, physical education, and recess.

Many states now also require reading or language arts tests for high school students as well as state tests in mathematics and science.

We systematically reviewed middle and secondary reading test items from each of the 48 states that published test descriptions and/or had test items released for public review. In general, the tests are remarkably similar in form and content. As a group, state reading/language arts assessments for grades four through 12 can be described as timed assessments in which students read both fiction and nonfiction passages and then answer multiple-choice questions. Most of the states also have performance test items, which require students to respond in writing to the content of one or more passages. Most of the test items focus on either passage comprehension or recall of information and include vocabulary questions based on words found in the passages. A majority of the state reading assessments have visual literacy test items requiring interpretation of information from maps, charts, tables, and pictures. About a third of the assessments have test items devoted to locating information or using reference materials. Figure 4.1 is a summary showing the number and percentage of the 48 states with various test characteristics. For example, 36 of the states (75 percent) have some vocabulary test items on their state reading assessments.

Fig. 4.1. Summary of Reading Test Characteristics in 48 States

Test Characteristic	Number of States	Percentage of States
Multiple-Choice Items	48	100%
Fiction Passages	45	94%
Nonfiction Passages	45	94%
Passage Independent Items	39	81%
Performance Items	39	81%
Vocabulary Test Items	36	75%
Visual Literacy Questions	30	62%
Location of Information Items	18	38%
Separate Vocabulary Section	7	15%
Matching or True/False Items	0	0%

Are State Reading Assessments Valid?

Most of the tests have been developed for individual states so that they are coordinated with each state's standards for reading. The state assessments of reading are different from most nationally recognized standardized tests. The differences raise interesting questions about the validity of the state assessments and, at the same time, make them vulnerable to test preparation techniques.

Test Validity

An evaluation of test validity answers the question: "Does the test measure what it claims to measure?" In the case of reading tests, the assessments should measure reading ability and, to the extent possible, nothing else. There are, of course, no pure reading tests that can assess reading comprehension without also indirectly measuring prior knowledge and general intelligence. However, for the last 30 years, the authors of standardized reading tests have been scrupulous in their attempts to render standardized reading tests as pure as possible, however most of the current state assessments of reading include test items that make it unclear as to just exactly what is being measured by the "reading" tests. These items fall into two categories: performance items and passage independent items.

Performance Items

Performance items ask students to write short essays, for example, a brief summary, an evaluation of the author's purpose, or a prediction of events that go beyond the passage itself. Usually, the state has a rubric for scoring performance items. There is nothing wrong with assessing writing skills and encouraging writing across the curriculum. However, when an assessment that claims to test reading achievement includes performance items and does not provide separate scores for reading and writing, these two aspects of literacy are confounded, reducing the validity of the assessment. After all, it is possible to be a good reader and not a good writer.

Passage Dependence

A test item is *passage independent* if you can answer it without even reading the passage. If you have to read the passage in order to acquire the information to answer the question correctly, the test item is *passage dependent*. Reading tests become invalid when test items are passage independent because the questions can be answered based on prior knowledge and logic rather than on reading ability. To the extent that state assessments of reading contain passage independent items, they are measures of general knowledge or achievement instead of reading. Assume, for example, that Question 1 (on the following page) is based on a passage from a state reading assessment.

Question 1

Which of the following countries was a U.S. ally in World War II?

     A. England

     B. Japan

     C. Italy

     D. Germany

In this hypothetical case, you would certainly be able to answer the question without having to read the passage. The question would, therefore, be passage independent for you and irrelevant or misleading in any assessment of your reading ability. Instead, the item would assess knowledge of American history. Obviously, a question can be passage independent for one person and passage dependent for another. When a reading test contains too many questions that are passage independent, the test is measuring something besides reading ability.

State reading assessments are riddled with passage independent questions. Some questions are answerable based on general knowledge. Others are designed to test state standards but have formats that make the answer passage independent. For example, one of the standards common to most states, distinguishing fact from opinion, is assessed in Question 2 (on the following page) which can be answered without reading the passage. Word clues such as *might* in option *C* occur frequently in state reading assessments. This wording means that the answer is found in the question itself rather than in the passage.

Question 2

Which of the following statements expresses an opinion by the author?

    A. The civil war ended in 1865.

    B. John Brown died leading a slave revolt.

    C. The South might have won the war if Lee had prevailed at Gettysburg.

    D. The North had more trains and factories than the South.

Questions about vocabulary are another common form of passage independence in almost all state reading assessments. Multiple-choice items regularly include general vocabulary and technical terms taken from a passage. Typically, the words in the multiple-choice questions are not introduced in the passage as new vocabulary but are instead merely words that occur in the passage. Question 3 (below) is an example of an eighth-grade item.

Question 3

By using context clues, the reader can determine that the word *cower*, as in "cower behind me," means

    A. jump repeatedly.

    B. hide fearfully.

    C. crawl slowly.

    D. rise quickly.

Given the restrictions of time, it is unlikely that a student who did not already know the meaning of *cower* would be able to return to the passage, find the word, and then use context clues to decipher its meaning. This test item is, therefore, passage independent.

Conclusions

Based on our survey of released test items, state reading assessments for middle and secondary students are, in reality, assessments of reading ability, writing ability, and prior knowledge. This means that many of the tests are of questionable validity as reading assessments and are more like general achievement tests. However, it also means that a subject-oriented approach to reading to learn makes sense because art, English, foreign language, health, mathematics, music, science, and social studies teachers are the people who build the vocabulary and prior knowledge essential to improving scores on state reading assessments. The nature of the tests also makes it realistic for subject-area teachers to prepare students systematically for state assessments without sacrificing curriculum objectives.

Brain Break

Curiosity and Clarification

Do you believe that state assessments in reading and mathematics are a valid and useful component of the public school curriculum in your state? Why or why not? Discuss your response with other teachers.

Test Preparation for State Reading Assessments

There is, of course, nothing that will improve performance on state reading assessments more than improvement in your students' knowledge of American history, chemistry, English, health, and other subject areas. However, to prepare students for the format of the test, there are two general strategies you can use: mirror assessment and principles of testwiseness for multiple-choice tests.

Mirror Assessment

Mirror assessment refers to the practice of preparing classroom examinations in a format that reflects the format students will encounter on the state reading assessment. We are not suggesting that every test and quiz in every classroom should be a mirror assessment, but teachers should use some mirror assessments to guarantee proper practice and mental readiness for the state reading assessment. Most of the state assessments have the following format: text passages followed by multiple-choice questions followed by a short writing requirement (performance item). We recommend the following Mirror Assessment Strategy (MAS) for subject-area test development:

- Test items should be *multiple-choice* with four or five options, depending upon the format for your particular state. State reading assessments do not use true/false, matching, or other item formats. Items should include questions that reflect the reading standards for your state. For example, almost all states have a standard that requires students to distinguish fact from opinion and questions reflecting this standard are common among the test items released by the various states. If your subject area lends itself easily to this standard, you may want to include such questions.

- Include at least one performance item—*short essay*—that follows the rubric for your state.

- The test should be *open-book* so that students have an opportunity to search for information as they would in the state reading assessment.

- The test should be *timed* so that students develop the ability to pace themselves.

- Students should be required to bubble in answers to multiple-choice items on *standardized forms*.

Testwiseness

Testwiseness refers to a series of principles that can be applied to exams independently of subject-area knowledge. To be testwise is to be able to: (1) exploit the flaws in exams, and (2) apply logic, common sense, and good organization in test-taking situations.

There is no substitute for being knowledgeable. However, being testwise can help students to perform better on state reading assessments. The present discussion will be limited to testwiseness in taking multiple-choice tests.

When you are preparing students for Mirror Assessment Strategy tests or state assessments in reading, encourage them to do the following:

- Read all directions carefully. It is not unusual for students to get poor scores on exams simply because they fail to read and follow directions.

- Always guess if they do not know the answer. Students should never leave a multiple-choice question blank.

- Budget time so that they are certain to finish the test. Students sometimes spend too much time on one part of the test and then fail to finish another.

- Do not waste time on items that are very difficult. Students should take a guess and make a light mark in the test booklet—if this is permitted—and go back to the tough questions at the end of the exam. They should not leave answers blank along the way because it is easy to mark answers out of sequence on the answer sheet, which can result in devastating score reductions.

- Try to come up with the answer to the question before they look at the alternatives. By thinking of the answer first, students are less likely to be fooled by seductive foils.

- Look at all the answers before making a choice. Multiple-choice tests typically require students to select the *best* answer.

- If the right answer is not clear right away, try to eliminate obvious wrong or silly answers and then guess from among those that remain. For example:

  The speed of sound is:

  A. 3,700 feet per second

  B. 1,087 feet per second

  C. 0 feet per second

  D. 186 miles per second

Students should be able to eliminate answer *C* right away. This would give them a one in three chance of guessing right instead of a one in four chance.

- Whenever two of the options are identical, both answers must be wrong. For example:

The universal donor is:

    A. O

    B. H_2O

    C. AB

    D. water

In this example, *H2O* and *water* are the same. By eliminating choices *B* and *D*, students now have a 50/50 chance of choosing the right answer.

- Whenever two of the options are opposites, one of them is always wrong and the other is often, but not always, right. For example:

A *proton* is:

    A. a positively charged particle

    B. a free atom

    C. a negatively charged particle

    D. a displaced neutron

- Know that the answer to a question may appear in the stem of another question. For example, in the following items, the answer to item I can be found in the stem of item II.

    I. A z-score is a:

        A. percentile equivalent

        B. concept in criterion referenced testing

        C. measure of standard error

        D. standardized score

    II. Standardized scores such as z-scores and t-scores are based on:

        A. standard deviations

        B. stanines

        C. chi squares

        D. grade equivalents

- When guessing, select an answer that is neither the first nor the last. (**Note:** This is probably the *least* effective strategy because state assessments are made by professional test designers, who randomize the options.)

Brain Break

Curiosity and Clarification

Generate one curiosity or clarification question about test preparation. Discuss your statement with other teachers.

Summary

The United States federal government requires that all states do systematic evaluations of students' reading skills. The various state assessments of reading ability tend to reflect state standards and are quite similar in format. Many state reading assessments are of questionable validity as reading achievement tests because they have writing requirements and passage independent questions that measure prior knowledge as well as reading ability. The nature of the state reading assessments is such that they lend themselves to successful test preparation strategies by classroom teachers.

Reflections on 21st Century Learning

1. Evaluate your current test preparation strategies or determine if you need to include test preparation strategies in your curriculum. How can you show students the difference between passage independent questions and questions that require them to return to the text?

2. How can you incorporate more test practice into your daily curriculum in an authentic way?

Overview of Research-Based Strategies

The research-based strategies we recommend have shown by specific studies to improve reading and learning. In other cases, the strategies are based on documented psychological processes and are designed to increase attention during reading or to improve the retention of new information. See the Related Readings in Appendix D for additional information about these strategies.

In Chapter 1, we introduced the notion that maximizing the results of reading to learn requires pre-reading preparation, guidance in searching for selected ideas during reading, and post-reading reinforcement of new vocabulary and subject area concepts. The remaining chapters contain strategies for improving content area reading. We trust that you will have an opportunity to experiment with them in your classrooms. Be patient! Don't expect instant results the first time you use a recommended strategy. First attempts at strategy implementation are problematic. Results will come with time and repeated efforts. Note that some strategies work well with particular content areas or may work better for particular units within a content area. Your professional judgment should guide strategy selection and use. Try a strategy several times before you render a final judgment on its added value.

The chapters are structured to facilitate your instructional planning. The elements are presented in a common format designed to assist you in your initial selection of reading strategies. Each chapter then concludes with Reflections on 21st Century Learning to help you consider instruction using these strategies.

The organizational features of each chapter are:

- **Description:** The description is a one- or two-paragraph summary of the strategy.

- **Timing:** Check marks indicate whether the strategy is designed for pre-reading, during reading, as a post-reading exercise, or as some combination of these. The example below suggests that the strategy would be useful as either a pre-reading or post-reading activity.

  - ☑ Pre-reading
  - ☐ During Reading
  - ☑ Post-reading

- **Logistics:** For each strategy, we have used bubbles to indicate how much extra time might be required for teacher preparation, how much in-class instructional time the activity might consume, and the complexity of the strategy for students. An empty bubble means not time consuming or complex; a half-filled bubble indicates somewhat time-consuming or complex; and a full bubble means the teacher should allow plenty of extra time or consider this activity very complex. Obviously, these can only be estimates and will vary widely by the age and disposition of students as well as by content area. The example below shows an activity with a high level of complexity, requiring little teacher preparation time and a moderate amount of instructional time.

  - ○ Teacher preparation time
  - ◑ Instructional time
  - ● Complexity

- **Targets:** Each strategy should encourage students to become better readers or more sophisticated learners by targeting a specific skill or set of skills. Of the five primary targets, those that are best matched to the strategy are checked. In the example below, the strategy is best suited to *expand or restructure knowledge* and *enhance learning and memory.*

  ☐ Increase fluency

  ☐ Increase attention during reading

  ☐ Utilize prior knowledge to facilitate comprehension

  ☑ Expand or restructure knowledge

  ☑ Enhance learning and memory

- **Directions:** Each strategy is presented with step-by-step instructions and usually includes an example. Some of the strategies include a blank template, which you are free to reproduce for noncommercial purposes in order to reduce preparation time.

Strategies for Developing Vocabulary

Academic vocabulary takes on special importance as students grapple with content-area texts. The growing number of ELL students, struggling readers, and students accustomed to telegraphic forms of text (e.g., text messaging) are likely to benefit from the guidance you can offer in helping them develop ownership of academic vocabulary in the content areas. Each of the following strategies provides a foundation for learning and using the insider's language of a discipline:

- Personal Glossary

- R^3 (Rehearsal, Rehearsal, Rehearsal)

- Contextual Redefinition

- Possible Sentences

- Verbal and Visual Word Association

- Clues and Questions

- Semantic Mapping

- Etymologia

- Morphologia

- Feature Analysis

Personal Glossary

Description

A *Personal Glossary* is a strategy to aid students' long-term memory of words which are novel or with which they have had difficulty. These can be words introduced by the teacher or words which students encounter on their own. The Personal Glossary need not be elaborate and should follow the format of a regular text glossary, with minor modifications.

Timing	Logistics
☐ Pre-reading	◑ Teacher preparation time
☑ During Reading	◑ Instructional time
☑ Post-reading	◑ Complexity

Targets

☐ Increase fluency

☐ Increase attention during reading

☐ Utilize prior knowledge to facilitate comprehension

☑ Expand or restructure knowledge

☑ Enhance learning and memory

Personal Glossary Directions

1. **Introduce the glossary format.** While the standard dictionary format is comprehensive, it may present more features than are necessary for students' personal glossaries.

We recommend the following components for a personal glossary:

    a. the word

    b. its definition

    c. a sentence using the word in context

The pronunciation of the word, its part of speech, and/or its etymology may be useful for your students. Introduce the format you want your students to use and show them how the personal glossaries should look. For example, figure 5.1 shows the target word, *bonfire*, in a Personal Glossary entry.

Fig. 5.1. Personal Glossary

> **Word**: *bonfire*
>
> **Definition**: large fire built in the open air
>
> **Sentence**: The football team built a bonfire at its party to celebrate its victory over its main rival.

2. **Direct students in the glossary's usage.** The personal glossary is used individually by students to help them retain word meanings. Students should enter those words introduced by you that are difficult for them, as well as problematic words they encounter in their own class reading. Explain that the glossaries are their responsibility to maintain; emphasize the importance of the glossaries in helping students learn and retain key vocabulary words and their meanings, particularly for a test. Demonstrate that students can use the words to quiz themselves about the definitions and how to use the words in a sentence. Emphasize that they can make the words a part of their permanent vocabulary through periodic rehearsal of each word's definition and use in context.

R³ (Rehearsal, Rehearsal, Rehearsal)

Description

R^3 is the pre-reading strategy we used to introduce new vocabulary in the preceding chapters. Its purpose is to add prior knowledge and increase the probability that the reader's attention will be focused on the most important vocabulary when those new words are encountered during the reading assignment.

Timing

☑ Pre-reading

☐ During Reading

☐ Post-reading

Logistics

◑ Teacher preparation time

◑ Instructional time

○ Complexity

Targets

☑ Increase fluency

☐ Increase attention during reading

☐ Utilize prior knowledge to facilitate comprehension

☑ Expand or restructure knowledge

☑ Enhance learning and memory

R³ (Rehearsal, Rehearsal, Rehearsal) Directions

1. **Identify the crucial vocabulary.** List and define the words you want students to focus on the most during a reading assignment.

2. **Present the words for rehearsal.** Using an overhead, document camera, interactive whiteboard, or other device present the new vocabulary and ask students to read each word three times in succession followed by a single reading of the definition. Depending upon the age and disposition of the group, this activity can be silent and individual, or done as a chorus with the whole class participating.

Contextual Redefinition

Description

Contextual redefinition is a strategy that introduces new vocabulary in rich contexts, which helps to define words and facilitate memory by giving the words meaningful associations. Students gain several benefits from this strategy. First, they realize that trying to identify an unfamiliar word by simply focusing on the word as an isolated element is frustrating, makes for haphazard guessing, and probably is not very accurate. Consequently, they are prompted to develop more reliable methods for determining meaning. Second, students become actively involved in a more profitable process of discovering new words rather than in the rote memorization of them. Third, the dictionary is cast in its most appropriate role—that of a tool used to verify the meanings of unfamiliar words by selecting the definition that is syntactically and semantically acceptable in a particular context. Since the components of contextual redefinition are familiar, we recommend this strategy for its simplicity and ease for content teachers.

Timing
- ☑ Pre-reading
- ☐ During Reading
- ☐ Post-reading

Logistics
- ◑ Teacher preparation time
- ◑ Instructional time
- ● Complexity

Targets
- ☐ Increase fluency
- ☐ Increase attention during reading
- ☑ Utilize prior knowledge to facilitate comprehension
- ☑ Expand or restructure knowledge
- ☑ Enhance learning and memory

Contextual Redefinition Directions

1. **Select unfamiliar words.** Identify those words that may present trouble to your students and that may be central to understanding the important concepts they will encounter in their reading. Select only a few words to be presented at one time to prevent the lesson from becoming tedious. To illustrate contextual redefinition, we will use the following words:

   carapace

   nonsectarian

   insipid

2. **Write a sentence.** Create an appropriate context for each word with clues to its meaning. If such a context already exists in the text material the students are about to read, it is appropriate to use that in lieu of creating a new context for it. If you need to create a context, be sure to use a variety of context clues (e.g., previous experience, compare/contrast, description) in the writing of these sentences. Specifically, a context clue related to previous experience provides an idea of which students will have knowledge because of their prior life experiences. A compare/contrast context clue offers similarities and dissimilarities related to the word in question. Finally, description context clues give a representation or an account of the new vocabulary word.

   carapace: Without its *carapace*, the turtle would be subject to certain death from its enemies or the elements.

   nonsectarian: Although he was a believer in God, he had a *nonsectarian* attitude toward religion.

   insipid: She had presented her lesson in a dull manner, failing to challenge or stimulate the students. The teacher knew she had made an *insipid* presentation.

In the sample sentences provided, *carapace* could be identified by previous experience, *nonsectarian* by compare and contrast, and *insipid* by description.

3. **Present the words in isolation.** Using the board or a transparency, ask students to provide you with a meaning for the unfamiliar word using only their prior knowledge. Some guesses may be off base or even humorous, but students should be asked to decide which of the offered meanings is the best. If students are working in small groups, each team could offer its best guess about the meaning.

4. **Present the words in a sentence.** Using the sentence you developed previously, present the word using the clues provided by the surrounding context to help supply a meaning. It is important that students who volunteer definitions defend their guesses by identifying the clues they used. In this way, struggling readers will be able to experience the thinking processes of other students and how they arrive at a meaning. In essence, students can act as models for one another.

5. **Dictionary verification.** A volunteer or volunteers who act as "dictionary judges" can look up the word in a print or online dictionary to verify the guesses offered by the class. This step also provides students and the teacher an opportunity to examine any morphemes or meaningful word parts present in the word and how they might help in its verification.

6. **Add words to a personal glossary.** Finally, to aid in long-term memory, students can add particularly difficult words to their personal glossaries.

Possible Sentences

Description

Possible Sentences is a strategy that helps students use technical vocabulary and related concepts (Stahl and Kapinus 1991). This strategy places students in an active role in which they predict an author's use of language in a text and evaluate their written predictions against the actual text passage. Possible sentences give students a purpose for reading the text by focusing their attention on the vocabulary words to be learned.

Timing

- ☑ Pre-reading
- ☑ During Reading
- ☑ Post-reading

Logistics

- ○ Teacher preparation time
- ◐ Instructional time
- ◐ Complexity

Targets

- ☐ Increase fluency
- ☐ Increase attention during reading
- ☑ Utilize prior knowledge to facilitate comprehension
- ☑ Expand or restructure knowledge
- ☑ Enhance learning and memory

Possible Sentences Directions

1. **List words.** On the white board or a transparency, list key terms from the reading selection. The words should be well defined by the context and pronounced several times for the students. Our example words are:

   - *pigment*   - *enzymes*   - *suntan*

   - *albinism*   - *melanin*   - *albino*

These words have been drawn from the following passage.

Albinism

The absence of pigmentation in the skin, hair, and eyes in albinos is the result of a deficiency in the manufacture of pigment (*melanin*) by the body. Albinism is a metabolic disorder resulting from the absence or inactivity of a specific enzyme. Enzymes are complex compounds that act as catalytic agents or mediators of chemical changes in living forms. This enzyme is involved in the formation of melanin. The condition is not restricted to humans. It has been found in many animals including snakes, salamanders, gorillas, rats, mice, bunnies, and even ravens, to name a few.

Human albinos are characterized by white translucent skin and white hair. Because of the lack of pigment in the iris, the eyes are red due to blood vessels. There is no way to overcome albinism. The necessary information to produce the right enzyme has not been inherited and will never be acquired. The specific enzyme or the melanin pigment would have to be injected

---

Albinism *(cont.)*

continuously into each and every pigment cell of the skin, scalp, and eyes in order to produce a normally pigmented individual. Albinos need continuous protection from sunlight since they burn very easily. Their skin cannot develop a suntan since tans are nothing more than the accumulation of melanin as a response to an increase in the ultraviolet radiation of sunlight. They are also more susceptible to skin diseases and tend to have poor vision. They are otherwise perfectly normal people.

(Brum, Castro, and Quinn 1978)

2. **Elicit sentences.** Individual students select any two of the words and dictate or write a sentence using them. The teacher writes the sentences on the board exactly as dictated, whether the information in them is accurate or inaccurate. For example:

Possible Sentences

a. Suntans come from having a lot of enzymes in skin.

b. An albino is a person who has no melanin.

c. An albino can never get a suntan.

d. Albinism is the missing of pigment in the skin.

3. **Verify sentences.** After an arbitrary number of sentences have been generated, the students search through the passage to verify the sentences on the board. A game twist can be added to this by having teams that are supposed to generate as many sentences as possible with unique pairs of the words listed. In this example, there are 15 different possible pairs of words that can be used. Once each team generates its sentences, the opposing teams challenge (with

books open or closed, at your discretion) the accuracy of each set of individual sentences. Points can be given for each accurate sentence. Penalty points can be deducted for inaccurate challenges.

4. **Revise Sentences.** The possible sentences are corrected on the board and students are given an opportunity to enter them into their personal glossaries. For example:

Revised Possible Sentences

a. Suntans come from having a lot of melanin in your skin.

b. An albino is a person who has no melanin.

c. An albino can never get a suntan.

d. Albinism is the absence of pigment in the skin.

Possible sentences will filter out any misconceptions students have about a topic. Writing sentences is generally a non-threatening activity, even for English language learners. We have found that students enthusiastically pursue text reading to verify their predictions.

Verbal and Visual Word Association

Description

Verbal and Visual Word Association is designed to capitalize on the word meanings students already know through their previous experiences to help them learn and retain new general and technical vocabulary (Hopkins and Bean 1999). It can be introduced to students easily and works best for nouns and descriptive adjectives. It is especially effective for struggling readers and, with adaptations, for English language learners in content-area classes. Given some guided practice, it should quickly become part of their repertoire of independent strategies for learning new vocabulary.

Timing

- ☑ Pre-reading
- ☑ During Reading
- ☐ Post-reading

Logistics

- ○ Teacher preparation time
- ◑ Instructional time
- ○ Complexity

Targets

- ☐ Increase fluency
- ☐ Increase attention during reading
- ☑ Utilize prior knowledge to facilitate comprehension
- ☑ Expand or restructure knowledge
- ☑ Enhance learning and memory

Fig. 5.2. Word Association Template

Word Association Diagram

Directions: Use this strategy to help you remember the meanings of new words.

1. In the top left box, write the new word.

2. In the bottom left box, write a short definition of the new word.

3. In the top right box, give an example of the word or something about the word that you think is important.

4. In the bottom right box, give a non-example of the new word.

New Word	Example or description
Definition	Non-example

Verbal and Visual Word Association Directions

1. **Create the word association diagram.** First, draw a blank square with four boxes in it. Ask students to make a copy of this diagram in their personal glossaries. Write the new word in the top left box. (The template shown in figure 5.2 on the previous page represents a schematic drawing of a word association diagram and its component parts to guide you in using this strategy.)

2. **Use the context and provide a definition** for the word in the bottom left box.

3. **Generate an example or description.** Students should generate a personal association for the word—something from their own lives. Have each student write that word in the upper right box.

4. **Generate a non-example.** In the lower right box, have students include a word that describes something they do or something they experience that is not an example of the word. These verbal associations can be used to study and retain a personally meaningful conception of the word.

Suppose students are reading along in a novel and encounter the following passage:

> *Joan had recently taken up jogging. She used to live life in the fast lane—staying out all night dancing and partying till dawn. Now that she was middle-aged, Joan strived for a more* salubrious *lifestyle.*

The word *salubrious* is a general vocabulary term that is not well known by most students. See figure 5.3 on page 94 for a completed word association diagram for the word *salubrious*.

Fig. 5.3. Word Association Diagram for *salubrious*

New Word	Example or description
Salubrious	Daily Vitamin
Definition	**Non-example**
Promoting Health	Smoking

English language learners may benefit from a modification of the original verbal association strategy. By including a visual association with the verbal symbol and omitting the non-example, English language learners can quickly grasp unfamiliar vocabulary. For example, the word *nocturnal* can be associated with the drawing of a half moon and stars against a black background (see figure 5.4) and placed in the lower right box.

Fig. 5.4. Word Association Diagram for *nocturnal*

New Word	Example or description
Nocturnal	Owl
Definition	**Visual example**
Active at Night	

Clues and Questions

Description

Clues and Questions is a strategy designed to help students review technical vocabulary. What makes clues and questions interesting is the fact that students provide the questions as well as the answers. As a vocabulary builder, the clues and questions strategy has a number of strengths. First, allowing students to create their own questions for a game gives them a novel purpose for using the text. Second, students will benefit from trying to write clear and meaningful questions. And third, participating in the vocabulary review itself will enlarge and reinforce students' technical vocabularies.

Timing
- ☐ Pre-reading
- ☐ During Reading
- ☑ Post-reading

Logistics
- ◑ Teacher preparation time
- ◑ Instructional time
- ○ Complexity

Targets
- ☐ Increase fluency
- ☐ Increase attention during reading
- ☐ Utilize prior knowledge to facilitate comprehension
- ☑ Expand or restructure knowledge
- ☑ Enhance learning and memory

Clues and Questions Directions

1. **Select the words for review.** Collect content-area vocabulary for students to review. Write each term on a note card and place it in a shoebox or card file. Or, if students have access to an interactive whiteboard or a laptop, the words can be stored in a database.

2. **Have students write questions.** Students randomly select vocabulary cards and write questions that can be answered by each word. Students can use the textbook index to find where the words are used. Give examples of different kinds of questions and clues (e.g., definition, analogy, compare and contrast, context) and encourage students to vary their question formats. Check the questions for accuracy. Have students print them on the vocabulary card directly below the word or in their database collections. Below are sample questions created for the vocabulary word *molecule*.

   a. _____ is to compound as atom is to element.

   b. What is the smallest unit of a compound that retains all the characteristics of that compound?

   c. Two hydrogen atoms and one oxygen atom make one _____ of water.

3. **Conduct the vocabulary review.** Have students work in small groups. Give each group a portion of the vocabulary cards. One student selects a card but does not look at it. Other students ask questions or supply a clue until the word is identified. Students take turn until the cards have been used. Students exchange cards and begin anew.

Semantic Mapping

Description

Semantic Mapping is a strategy which utilizes a diagram that groups related concepts (Heimlich and Pittelman 1986). Semantic maps may be used as pre-reading or post-reading exercises that reinforce new vocabulary and help students relate their prior knowledge to new experiences and concepts. Semantic mapping lends itself well to a small group instructional format.

Timing

☑ Pre-reading

☐ During Reading

☑ Post-reading

Logistics

○ Teacher preparation time

◑ Instructional time

○ Complexity

Targets

☐ Increase fluency

☐ Increase attention during reading

☐ Utilize prior knowledge to facilitate comprehension

☑ Expand or restructure knowledge

☑ Enhance learning and memory

Semantic Mapping Directions

1. **Select a topic.** Select an important word or topic from the reading assignment. Our example topic is based on disastrous volcanoes. The topic in this case will be *volcano* and is written on the board or a transparency.

2. **Generate related words.** Assign students to write down as many related words or phrases as they can think of from their own experiences and/or from their reading of the text. In this case, we will assume that students have read the text.

Mount Vesuvius	*Vulcanian*	*Pompeii*
Mount St. Helens	*cataclysm*	*lava*
ash	*earthquake*	*ring of fire*
vent	*conduit*	*volcanic bombs*
gas	*blocks*	*tsunami*
explosions	*plug*	*Krakatoa*
pressure	*hell*	*terrifying*
plate tectonics	*magma*	*shield*

3. **Generate word groups.** Ask students to examine the words in the large list and have them make smaller groupings of words that are related to one another in some way. Tell them to give these categories of words a label that describes how they are related.

4. **Create the diagram.** Organize the words into a diagram by asking students to share their word groups while you write them on the board. As new categories emerge, give the map new arms or add categories of your own. The diagram itself can be as simple or as complex as you desire. There is no one correct diagram. One possibility is shown in figure 5.5.

Fig. 5.5. Semantic Map Using the Topic *Volcano*

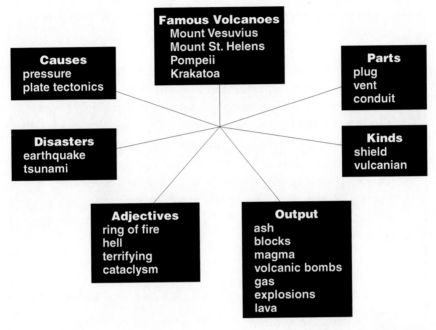

Bean, Readence, and Baldwin 2008

5. **Follow up.** Perhaps the most important step in this activity is the discussion and questioning activities designed to reinforce the new concepts in the diagram. For example:

   a. Why are volcanoes considered disastrous?

   b. Which do you think was the all-time most disastrous volcano?

   c. Why is "ring of fire" a good name?

   d. In what ways are Mauna Loa and Mount Vesuvius different? How are they the same?

   e. Tell what it would have been like to be on the island of Krakatoa in 1883.

   f. "Mark, imagine that you are Krakatoa. Susan, imagine that you are Mount St. Helens. Now, each of you should try to convince the other that you are the world's greatest volcano."

Etymologia

Description

Etymologia is a strategy for building and reinforcing word meanings by investigating the etymologies or histories of words. If a word has interesting associations with other words and scripts, there is an enhanced probability that the word will be remembered. The word *sabotage,* for example, should be easier for students to remember if they also know that *sabots* are wooden shoes, and that workers in Holland during the Industrial Revolution threw their sabots into machinery as a means of protesting working conditions. Stories like that stick in the mind.

Timing
- ☑ Pre-reading
- ☐ During Reading
- ☑ Post-reading

Logistics
- ○ Teacher preparation time
- ◐ Instructional time
- ◐ Complexity

Targets
- ☐ Increase fluency
- ☐ Increase attention during reading
- ☐ Utilize prior knowledge to facilitate comprehension
- ☑ Expand or restructure knowledge
- ☑ Enhance learning and memory

Etymologia Directions

1. **Select the words.** Identify the crucial vocabulary in upcoming reading assignments.

2. **Assign students.** On a rotating basis, assign students in teams of two to find as many interesting etymologies as possible for the words that have been assigned to them. Students should be searching for stories they can share with their classmates prior to the corresponding reading assignment. In addition to library and print sources, have students use online search strategies to identify key stories and video clips that may make word meanings more memorable by association with historical events.

The prepared exercise shown in figure 5.6 on the next page, shows students how to find etymologies using classroom or library resources.

Fig. 5.6. Learning About Etymologies

Directions: The following words, listed by subject area, have interesting word origins. Use an unabridged dictionary, an etymological dictionary, an online source, or a book on interesting word origins to determine their histories. Your school librarian or media specialist should be able to help you find good reference books, dictionaries, and online sources. Write down the etymology of each word. Which words have the most interesting histories?

Science	Social Studies
alkali _____ _____	assassin _____ _____
cobalt _____ _____	boycott _____ _____
hurricane _____ _____	indenture _____ _____
nicotine _____ _____	senate _____ _____
Language Arts	**Mathematics**
tragedy _____ _____	division _____ _____
quixotic _____ _____	pi _____ _____
fib _____ _____	numeral _____ _____
dumbbell _____ _____	multiple _____ _____

Bean, Readence, and Baldwin 2008

Morphologia

Description

Morphologia is a strategy derived from the word *morpheme*. The strategy involves reviewing the morphemes that make up subject-area vocabulary as a means of increasing the number and diversity of associations with the word (Rasinski et al. 2008). This is very different from having students memorize hundreds of Latin and Greek roots and affixes to figure out the meanings of new words as they encounter them. Most of the Latinate words in English were constructed 500 to 1,000 years ago, so it is a rare occasion when simply adding the meanings of roots and affixes (morphemes) together will give you the current meaning of the word. On the other hand, if you are learning a new word and are exposed at the same time to the meanings of some of its parts, the morphemes will act as mnemonic devices for remembering the meaning of the associated word.

Timing

- ☑ Pre-reading
- ☐ During Reading
- ☑ Post-reading

Logistics

- ◑ Teacher preparation time
- ◑ Instructional time
- ● Complexity

Targets

- ☐ Increase fluency
- ☐ Increase attention during reading
- ☐ Utilize prior knowledge to facilitate comprehension
- ☑ Expand or restructure knowledge
- ☑ Enhance learning and memory

Morphologia Directions

1. **Explain the value of morphemes.** Tell students that knowing the meanings of word parts will help them to remember important words in your class. If they do not already have the knowledge, show students how to use a standard dictionary or online dictionary to find the meanings of morphemes in individual words.

2. **Illustrate the strategy.** Tell students that they are going to figure out what is the longest word in a standard dictionary. Place the word *pneumonoultramicroscopicsilicovolcanoconiosis* on a whiteboard or a *Microsoft PowerPoint*® slide and ask students if they know what it means. Or, you could use any complex word from your subject area. Ask the students then to search within the word for smaller parts for which they do know the meaning. Some of these—listed on the following page—are easier than others, so students may or may not need some help. Relate the word parts to words with similar meaning, for example, *pneumonia* and *osteoporosis*, as you gradually break the word down into parts.

pneumono/ultra/micro/scopic/silico/volcano/coni/osis

> *pneumono:* related to the lungs

> *ultra:* transcending; super

> *micro:* small

> *scopic:* related to a viewing instrument

> *silico:* the mineral, silicon

> *volcano:* eruption in the earth from which molten rock, steam, and dust issue

> *coni:* dust

> *osis:* referring to a diseased condition

Ultimately, you should be able to lead students to understand that *pneumonoultramicroscopicsilicovolcanoconiosis* is a disease of the lungs caused by habitual inhalation of very fine silicon dust particles. Chances are students will not forget this word.

3. **Explain the strategy.** The strategy is for students and/or the teacher to identify some or all of the morphemes in complex words and for students to list those meanings, along with the meanings of the words themselves, in their personal glossaries. Having whipped the longest word in English, learning the rest should be a piece of cake.

Feature Analysis

Description

Feature Analysis is a procedure that can help students make fine discriminations among concepts (Anders and Bos 1986). With respect to technical vocabulary, feature analysis can summarize distinctive ways in which related concepts are similar and different. With respect to general vocabulary, the procedure works well for teaching word connotations.

Timing	Logistics
☑ Pre-reading	◐ Teacher preparation time
☐ During Reading	● Instructional time
☑ Post-reading	◐ Complexity

Targets

☐ Increase fluency

☐ Increase attention during reading

☑ Utilize prior knowledge to facilitate comprehension

☑ Expand or restructure knowledge

☑ Enhance learning and memory

Feature Analysis Directions

1. **Select a category.** The category should be one that consists of two or more items that are similar. Such categories could be things like kinds of animals, elements, foods, famous historical characters, or words that have the same denotation but different connotations. We will use *planets* as our example category.

2. **List category terms.** Place the terms along the left-hand side of the board or transparency. Try not to use a large number of items the first time you use the procedure. In our example, we are looking at the similarities and differences among the planets in our solar system.

Mercury	Jupiter
Venus	Saturn
Earth	Uranus
Mars	Neptune

3. **List features.** Place the features that will be used to describe the terms (planets) across the top of the board. Students may select the features, or you may do it yourself. If you ask the students to provide the features, be prepared to give them plenty of hints and directions. Figure 5.7 shows a feature analysis chart for planets.

Fig. 5.7. Feature Analysis Chart

Category: Planets							
	Hot	Cold	Big	Small	Rings	Life	Moons
Mercury							
Venus							
Earth							
Mars							
Jupiter							
Saturn							
Uranus							
Neptune							

Baldwin, Readence, and Bean 2004

4. **Complete a feature analysis chart.** Students should be guided through the matrix as they indicate whether each category item possesses a given feature. This can be done individually, in a group, or in categories item by item. A plus sign (+) shows that the item has a selected feature. A minus sign (-) indicates that the item does not have the feature. Every item must have a plus or a minus for every feature; there should be no blank spots. In general, a plus sign indicates that a category item usually or mostly has that given feature. The presence of two minuses can indicate a third category. For example, if a planet is neither large nor small, then it is probably medium-size. Figure 5.8 represents our completed feature analysis chart for the category *planets*.

Fig. 5.8. Completed Feature Analysis Chart for Planets

Category: Planets							
	Hot	Cold	Big	Small	Rings	Life	Moons
Mercury	+	–	–	+	–	–	–
Venus	+	–	–	–	–	–	–
Earth	–	–	–	–	–	+	+
Mars	–	–	–	+	–	–	+
Jupiter	–	+	+	–	+	–	+
Saturn	–	+	+	–	+	–	+
Uranus	–	+	+	–	+	–	+
Neptune	–	–	+	–	+	–	+

Baldwin, Readence, and Bean 2004

5. **Explore the chart.** For the purpose of a review, the final step is to have the students make observations about the chart. However, questions and hints may be necessary. For example, here are some questions that can be answered based on the information in the *planets* chart. The questions are arranged from simple to complex:

   a. Which planets are the hottest?

   b. Which planets have rings?

   c. In what ways are Neptune and Mercury different?

   d. What makes Earth unique among the planets?

   e. Which planet is most like Earth? Why?

An enterprising student might argue that Mercury, because it has no atmosphere and does not rotate in its orbit around the sun, is half cold and half hot, in which case Mercury should be marked (+) in both the hot and cold columns. This sort of reasoning should be welcomed, along with divergent comments, changes in categories, and other student interactions. When conducted in a thoughtful and flexible manner, feature analysis is a good way to build and reinforce vocabulary.

Reflections on 21st Century Learning

1. How do you currently address academic vocabulary in your classroom?

2. Which of the vocabulary strategies in this chapter would you like to incorporate in your teaching? Why?

3. How do you see these strategies assisting ELL students in your classroom?

4. How do you see these strategies assisting struggling readers?

Strategies for Improving Comprehension

Students' comprehension of challenging content-area texts and online material will benefit from your careful scaffolding of how to read and understand this material. Moreover, students are reading multiple texts that require special attention to integrate ideas and concepts spanning both print and Internet sources. The strategies described in this chapter are designed to help your students meet these challenges:

- Anticipation/Reaction Guides

- KWL

- Think Alouds

- Quick Writes

- Mini Study Guides

- Text Appetizers

- Graphic Organizers

- Doodle Diagrams

Anticipation/Reaction Guide

Description

An *Anticipation/Reaction Guide* provides a window into students' prior knowledge and misconceptions about a topic, as well as an opportunity to revise initial points of view after reading an assignment. An anticipation/reaction guide consists of a series of brief statements with which the reader is asked to agree or disagree. These statements should be designed to encourage curiosity and controversy.

Timing	Logistics
☑ Pre-reading	◑ Teacher preparation time
☑ During Reading	◑ Instructional time
☑ Post-reading	○ Complexity

Targets

☐ Increase fluency

☑ Increase attention during reading

☑ Utilize prior knowledge to facilitate comprehension

☑ Expand or restructure knowledge

☑ Enhance learning and memory

Anticipation/Reaction Guide Directions

1. **Identify major concepts.** Identify the major concepts and supporting details in a text or non-print media selection.

2. **Identify experiences and beliefs.** Identify students' experiences and beliefs that will be challenged or supported by the material.

3. **Create anticipation/reaction statements.** Create three to five statements and arrange them on a sheet of paper, overhead transparency, or *Microsoft PowerPoint®* slide. The statements should be challenging and interesting and should require thinking at all levels of comprehension.

4. **Present the guide.** Have students respond positively or negatively to each statement on an individual basis. Have them record their justification for each response in writing, so they will have a reference point for future discussion.

5. **Prereading discussion.** Engage students in a prereading disc-ussion highlighting their current justification for responding positively or negatively to each statement. Do not reveal the answers to the class. Students should be encouraged to find the answers from their reading.

6. **Post-reading evaluation.** After the reading, have students respond again to each statement.

7. **Post-reading discussion.** In addition to having the correct information, the discussion should also focus on the restructuring of prior knowledge and the reasons behind changes in responses based on the reading.

Anticipation/Reaction Guides help target students' reading, guiding them toward an evaluation of existing beliefs and offering an opportunity to increase their content-area knowledge. They take relatively little teacher time to create, and the pay-off in student learning, interaction, and comprehension is well worth the effort. The example in figure 6.1 on the next page shows an Anticipation/ Reaction Guide on the topic of solar cars.

Fig. 6.1. Anticipation/Reaction Guide for Solar Cars

Directions: Read each statement. In the *Anticipation* column, circle *agree* or *disagree* and write your reason. After reading, reconsider your responses in the *Reaction* column.

Statement	Anticipation	Reaction
1. Solar cars must carry batteries to store solar energy.	*Agree Disagree* Reason:_____ _____	*Agree Disagree* Reason:_____ _____
2. Solar cars are unable to go faster than 20 miles per hour.	*Agree Disagree* Reason:_____ _____	*Agree Disagree* Reason:_____ _____
3. Solar cars need highly aerodynamic panels to capture solar energy.	*Agree Disagree* Reason:_____ _____	*Agree Disagree* Reason:_____ _____
4. Solar cars are barely able to carry one person.	*Agree Disagree* Reason:_____ _____	*Agree Disagree* Reason:_____ _____
5. I would rather have a gasoline-powered car than a solar car.	*Agree Disagree* Reason:_____ _____	*Agree Disagree* Reason:_____ _____

KWL

Description

KWL is an integrated strategy that encompasses and offers guidance in the three stages of a typical lesson: pre-reading, during reading, and post-reading. KWL can be thought of as an integrated approach to guiding students' comprehension of key content-area concepts in print and online material (Ogle 1986). KWL also serves a diagnostic function. By assessing what students currently know about a concept, you can quickly get an idea of their prior knowledge as well as any misconceptions they may have. KWL relies on three categories of information:

- **K**   What we *Know* (before reading)

- **W**   What we *Want* to find out (during reading)

- **L**   What we *Learned* (as a result of reading)

Timing

- ☑ Pre-reading
- ☑ During Reading
- ☑ Post-reading

Logistics

- ○ Teacher preparation time
- ◑ Instructional time
- ○ Complexity

Targets

- ☐ Increase fluency
- ☑ Increase attention during reading
- ☑ Utilize prior knowledge to facilitate comprehension
- ☑ Expand or restructure knowledge
- ☑ Enhance learning and memory

KWL Directions

1. **Brainstorm.** Have students brainstorm what they currently know about the topic. This information goes in the first of three columns, *K*, in a typical KWL lesson format.

2. **Create questions.** Have students create some questions that target their purpose for reading a selection. The questions go in the *W* column.

3. **Record information.** After reading, students can record in the *L* column information they have gleaned from their reading. Students may also generate another list of questions about what they *still* have to learn.

The KWL lesson framework and example in figure 6.2 illustrate a lesson took place in a biology class where the topic of adaptation evolved into a talk of killer bees and their successful migration across the United States. You may want to use small groups to complete the charts or sticky notes to add information to a large KWL chart developed by the class.

Fig. 6.2. KWL Chart

Killer Bees		
K	**W**	**L**
1. People die from them. 2. Dogs die from them.	1. Why are they called killer bees? 2. Where are they found? 3. How can we remove them?	1. They are very aggressive 2. Live in Southern and Western U.S. 3. Call an exterminator

Think Aloud

Description

Think Alouds are based upon a teacher-modeling approach wherein the teacher reads aloud from a text and verbalizes whatever comes to mind (Kucan and Beck 1997). This approach demystifies the reasoning that takes place during reading and may be used in conjunction with many other strategies for improving reading comprehension. Your verbalized thoughts may include questions, predictions, paraphrases, and evaluative statements.

Timing

- ☐ Pre-reading
- ☑ During Reading
- ☐ Post-reading

Logistics

- ○ Teacher preparation time
- ○ Instructional time
- ◑ Complexity

Targets

- ☐ Increase fluency
- ☐ Increase attention during reading
- ☑ Utilize prior knowledge to facilitate comprehension
- ☑ Expand or restructure knowledge
- ☐ Enhance learning and memory

Think Aloud Directions

1. **Passage selection.** Select a passage of between 100 and 300 words. The passage should be fairly difficult so that your reasoning is actually useful to the students. If the passage is too easy, students will not see the value of what you are doing. If your students are experiencing difficulty searching online resources effectively and getting lost in the process, use a think aloud to model the steps in searching efficiently. These steps include spelling keywords correctly, bookmarking website URLs so you can find information later, and carefully checking the credibility and trustworthiness of websites.

2. **Prepare think-aloud commentary.** Prepare your comments for the think aloud based on your experiences. Because the material will not be difficult for you, you need to plan an idealized set of think-aloud responses (pretend). You will be acting the part of a student with good reading and comprehension skills.

3. **Verbalize what you are doing.** Explain to the students exactly what you are doing; for example, say: "I am going to demonstrate my thoughts when I read a difficult text."

4. **Read.** Read the passage to the class and insert your planned think alouds as you go.

5. **Student questions.** When you are finished, give students a chance to ask you questions about your thinking or about the think-aloud procedure itself.

6. **Student practice.** Have students practice thinking aloud with smaller units of text.

The example in figure 6.3 provides an illustration of how a teacher models the think-aloud process with a text passage in social studies on Nigeria and various forms of imperialism. Italics show the teacher's inner thoughts verbalized during the think-aloud.

Fig. 6.3. Example of a Teacher's Think Aloud

Imperialism *(What does that mean?)* **and Colonial Control**

European nations varied in their policies and goals when they set out to establish colonies. For example, over time, four types of colonial control developed. The four colonial types are:

(a) **colony**—where a country is governed internally by a foreign power *(I think Somaliland in East Africa was a French colony, and this example helps me get a grip on the concept of colony).*

(b) **protectorate**—where a country or territory runs its own internal government under the control of an outside power *(I wonder if* protectorate *comes from* protect. *I think I'll check the etymology).*

(c) **sphere of influence**—*(like a circle on the map around a country)* where an outside power claims exclusive investment or trading rights

(d) **economic imperialism**—where private business interests control another country's industry *(I don't see how this term is different from the last one).*

Quick Write

Description

Quick Writes are an informal means of engaging students in thinking about a content topic during the pre-reading or post-reading stages of a lesson or unit. These short timed writing assignments are also useful as a mirror assessment strategy to prepare students for performance items on state reading assessments. Quick writes are typically based on teacher-generated questions. Students can jot down their ideas and share them with a partner or group or in their response journals for personal reflection. The teacher may also choose to collect them to provide constructive feedback; however—given the conditions of the writing—students should not be graded on quick writes.

Timing	Logistics
☑ Pre-reading	○ Teacher preparation time
☐ During Reading	○ Instructional time
☑ Post-reading	○ Complexity

Targets

☐ Increase fluency

☐ Increase attention during reading

☑ Utilize prior knowledge to facilitate comprehension

☑ Expand or restructure knowledge

☑ Enhance learning and memory

Quick Write Directions

1. **Generate pre-reading questions or issues.** The following writing prompts are designed to engage students in quick writes:

   - Before we begin our unit on water quality, write down everything you know about this topic. You will not be graded. You have one minute.

   - We are going to study recent efforts to achieve a Middle East peace accord. In 30 seconds, write down political figures who are likely to influence this effort.

2. **Generate post-reading questions or issues.** The writing prompts below are designed to help students reflect on readings or prepare for the state reading assessment:

   - Based on this reading assignment, what are the major ethical issues regarding the cloning of animals and human beings? You have one minute.

   - Today's math lesson dealt with statistical probability. Write down some examples from day-to-day life where knowing the statistical probability of an event might be important. You have three minutes.

3. **Evaluate.** If the purpose of quick writes is test preparation, you should apply whatever rubrics are available from the state and provide ungraded feedback to the students. Depending upon the age and sophistication of the class, the students may be able to do self-evaluations.

Quick writes are highly flexible so that the assignment can be adjusted to fit the time available. This is a great way to engage students in thinking about a topic before or after reading, and as a preparation for class discussion and performance items on state assessments. You can also use quick writes when you have a few minutes left in the class period, but if there is no feedback or discussion following quick writes, students may lose enthusiasm.

Mini Study Guide

Description

A *Mini Study Guide* is a set of questions and key vocabulary designed to focus student attention on those aspects of the text that are most important to you as the instructor. The questions should represent various levels of comprehension: text explicit (right on the page), text implicit (think-and-search), and experience based (on your own).

Timing
- ☐ Pre-reading
- ☑ During Reading
- ☐ Post-reading

Logistics
- ◑ Teacher preparation time
- ◑ Instructional time
- ◑ Complexity

Targets
- ☐ Increase fluency
- ☑ Increase attention during reading
- ☐ Utilize prior knowledge to facilitate comprehension
- ☑ Expand or restructure knowledge
- ☑ Enhance learning and memory

Mini Study Guide Directions

1. **Evaluate the material.** Identify the major concepts and important details in the reading assignment from which you will derive the questions.

2. **Write the questions.** Questions should cover the three levels of comprehension and should be ordered according to the location in the text where the answers to both text explicit and implicit questions will be found. This will cue students to backtrack if they find an answer when one or more of the preceding questions remains unanswered.

3. **Identify crucial vocabulary.** Adolescent readers are frequently overwhelmed by the number of new academic and general terms introduced in a reading assignment. Some of the new terms may be crucial from your point of view while others are of peripheral interest. It is quite useful to students to include in the mini study guide the new words and technical terms for which you will hold them responsible. Identify the selected crucial terms and list them in the order in which they occur in the text. It is possible to provide additional structure by giving students the page numbers where answers can be found; however, this may lead to skimming, as opposed to actual reading.

4. **Assign the guide.** Assign the mini study guide to accompany text reading and include follow-up discussion to check for comprehension.

The example in Figure 6.4 uses the topic of the American Revolution to illustrate the nature of questions created at multiple levels of comprehension.

Fig. 6.4. Mini Study Guide

The American Revolution

Right on the Page	Think-and-Search
1. What social and political changes occurred in the 13 colonies as a result of the American Revolution?	2. Why wasn't slavery abolished in the 1770s?

On Your Own	Vocabulary
3. Would you want to travel through time back to the 1770s during the drafting of the Constitution? Why or why not?	• Loyalist • Militia • Minutemen • Redcoats • Tory

Text Appetizer

Description

Text Appetizers are teacher-created, introductory paragraphs that offer a framework for comprehending a reading selection by relating the new to the known (e.g., connecting the new information in the text to prior knowledge common to the students). A Text Appetizer is also designed to build topic interest and to focus attention during reading.

Timing

- ☑ Pre-reading
- ☐ During Reading
- ☐ Post-reading

Logistics

- ◑ Teacher preparation time
- ○ Instructional time
- ○ Complexity

Targets

- ☐ Increase fluency
- ☑ Increase attention during reading
- ☑ Utilize prior knowledge to facilitate comprehension
- ☐ Expand or restructure knowledge
- ☐ Enhance learning and memory

Text Appetizer Directions

1. **Write the introductory paragraph.** Write an interest-building paragraph based on real life, day-to-day events that would be of interest to your students and are similar in principle to the critical target concepts in a text.

2. **Mini study guide** *(optional).* Add a Mini Study Guide (see figure 6.4).

3. **Read the text appetizer.** Have students read and discuss the appetizer before beginning the reading assignment. See figure 6.5 for a sample Text Appetizer.

Fig. 6.5. Text Appetizer

The Politics of Protest

Suppose you like to skateboard at the new skate park near your neighborhood. However, due to a small percentage of rowdy skateboarders causing trouble, the city council threatens to close down the skate park. What would you do about this situation?
The chapter you are about to read shows how groups such as small business people, workers, and farmers in the 1890s protested what they felt were unfair practices by big business, often with the support of the government. Farmers felt they were paying too much interest on equipment loans from big business banks. They banded together to protest this unfair treatment, just as you might protest lumping all skateboarders together despite only a small group causing problems at the skate park. Congress was viewed as a governmental body that could help the farmers with the plight, but, like many political systems, this one proved to have its flaws. As you read pages 537-549, try to answer the discussion questions below:

The American Revolution

Right on the Page	Think-and-Search
1. What was the purpose of the Sherman Antitrust Act?	**2.** Why did the Sherman Antitrust Act not work the way it was supposed to in 1890?
On Your Own	**Vocabulary**
3. Do you think the Sherman Antitrust Act is working today? Why or why not?	• protest • congress • governmental Body

Graphic Organizer

Description

Graphic Organizers are visual aids that define hierarchical relationships among concepts (Robinson 1998). They are an effective technique for introducing, reinforcing, and summarizing the major concepts in a reading assignment; they also lend themselves particularly well to the teaching of technical vocabulary.

Timing

- ☑ Pre-reading
- ☑ During Reading
- ☑ Post-reading

Logistics

- ◑ Teacher preparation time
- ◑ Instructional time
- ● Complexity

Targets

- ☐ Increase fluency
- ☐ Increase attention during reading
- ☐ Utilize prior knowledge to facilitate comprehension
- ☑ Expand or restructure knowledge
- ☑ Enhance learning and memory

Graphic Organizer Directions

1. **Concept identification.** An analysis of the content identifies all new terms and concepts that will be introduced in the reading assignment. Since there will often be a large number of these terms and concepts, it will save time simply to mark them in your own text.

The list in figure 6.6 below was derived from one chapter in a science text dealing with matter and how it is structured.

Fig. 6.6. Graphic Organizer for Matter

Matter

structure of matter	molecules	neutrons
elements	inert gases	energy levels
metals	natural elements	electrolysis
nucleus	compounds	positive electrical charge
mixtures	nonmetals	negative electrical charge
natural elements	atoms	electrons
particles	physical combination	chemical combination
protons	orbits	atomic theory of matter
electron shell	law of definite or constant proportions	

2. **Concept selection.** In order to prevent the organizer from being overly complex, it is critical to prune the initial list until it consists of only superordinate concepts, (e.g., those that are most essential to the integrity of the reading selection. The organizer is supposed to supplement the reading assignment, not replace it. Once the list has been reduced, subclassify the remaining terms in an informal outline as shown in Figure 6.7.

Fig. 6.7. Outline Based on Graphic Organizer

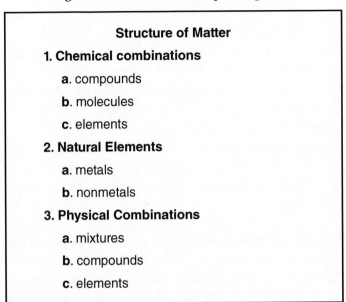

Structure of Matter

1. Chemical combinations

    a. compounds

    b. molecules

    c. elements

2. Natural Elements

    a. metals

    b. nonmetals

3. Physical Combinations

    a. mixtures

    b. compounds

    c. elements

3. Diagram construction. Arrange the terms in a tree diagram that reflects the structure established in Step 2 (see figure 6.8).

Fig. 6.8. Graphic Organizer on the Structure of Matter

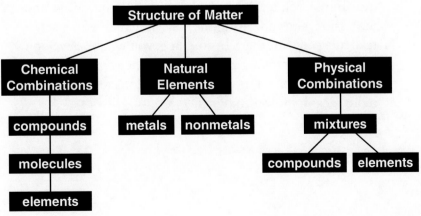

Baldwin, Readence, and Bean 2004

4. **Initial evaluation.** Once you have created the organizer, step back and evaluate it. Does the organizer accurately convey the concepts you wish to teach? If not, adjust the diagram until you are satisfied. One of the advantages of the graphic organizer is that it helps teachers to organize and clarify their own purposes. In addition to accuracy, consider the complexity of the diagram. Students can be overwhelmed if the visual display is too complicated. Under such conditions, it may be desirable to present the organizer piece-by-piece. Also, note that there are various software applications with digital approaches to constructing graphic organizers.

5. **Organizer presentation.** The physical presentation of the organizer is unimportant. Handouts, a permanent poster, *Microsoft PowerPoint*® slide, overhead transparency, or interactive whiteboard may be used as the teacher's resources dictate. The time required for the presentation will vary depending upon the complexity of the organizer and the extent to which the concepts in question are unfamiliar to students. Begin the presentation with a general explanation of the purpose of the organizer and an explanation of how a tree diagram works. Talk students through the organizer, explaining each term, encouraging student questions and discussion, and indicating the ways in which terms are related to one another. In so doing, you will be developing vocabulary, improving reading comprehension, and enriching schemata in ways which will make subject matter more meaningful to students.

Doodle Diagram

Description

Doodle Diagrams will help your students see how multiple texts on a topic can be compared and contrasted. Similar to Venn diagrams, Doodle Diagrams are based on students' drawings that are then filled in with words and concepts that compare and contrast an historical event, characters in a novel, or other content-area possibilities. This is a post-reading strategy in which the actual doodle will be keyed to the particular topic students are learning about. For example, in the illustration that follows, students are considering two contrasting views of Polynesian navigation theories that have been posed in the literature. In this case, students doodled two sailboats and listed concepts in the sail portion of their doodles. Making intertextual connections across multiple texts, including films, video clips, advertisements, and other media, is a fairly complex process. Therefore, you may want to begin by modeling this process using the think-aloud strategy described earlier in this chapter (page 117).

Timing

- ☐ Pre-reading
- ☐ During Reading
- ☑ Post-reading

Logistics

- ◑ Teacher preparation time
- ◑ Instructional time
- ● Complexity

Targets

- ☐ Increase fluency
- ☐ Increase attention during reading
- ☐ Utilize prior knowledge to facilitate comprehension
- ☑ Expand or restructure knowledge
- ☑ Enhance learning and memory

Doodle Diagram Directions

1. **Identify major concepts in two or more texts.** Identify the major concepts and supporting detail in two or more texts. For example, two very different views of the history of Polynesian navigation have been proposed. One view holds their travel from western Polynesia to Hawaii as a drifting process (e.g., the Kon Tiki raft's voyage). Another proposes a more sophisticated knowledge of how to use weather, stars, bird migration patterns, and so on to navigate to and from the Hawaiian Islands and elsewhere in the Pacific.

2. **Model the Doodle Diagram process.** In the case of this example, you could draw two sailboats and advise students that the key ideas and concepts in their reading of the two contrasting accounts of Polynesian navigation will go in the sail areas.

3. **Present the two texts.** The two texts offer contrasting views of Polynesian navigation across the Pacific to Hawaii. One view sees these voyages as primarily a process of accidentally drifting east while another view sees them as purposeful sailing windward, ultimately, to Hawaii.

4. **Students create their Doodle Diagrams and add concept labels.** Figures 6.9 through 6.12 on the following pages show one student's set of Doodle Diagrams for two reading passages.

Fig. 6.9. Text for Drift Theory

One prominent view of how Polynesia was settled rests on the common sense notion that voyagers and their double canoes drifted aimlessly in the Pacific, occasionally and accidentally reaching a landfall in places like the geographically remote Hawaiian Islands. Indeed, in 1947, anthropologist and explorer Thor Heyerdahl drifted from South America on a balsa log raft named Kon-Tiki. Drifting aimlessly downwind, voyagers, according to this theory, could only go in one direction. They were not able to sail back to their place of origin.

Fig. 6.10. Text for Intentional Voyaging

The intentional voyaging theory of Polynesian navigation posits that these double canoe sailors were able to use and read stars, bird migration patterns, cloud conditions, and ocean currents to sail off the westerly winds to remote islands like Hawaii and then return home to Tahiti. This theory has been well documented by the voyages of the double sailing canoe, Hokulea, in 1976, and later in 1980 with Hawaiian navigator, Nainoa Thompson, that voyage taking 33 days. These voyages show that Polynesian navigators could move thoughtfully across the expansive ocean to discover and settle new lands, even remote islands like Hawaii.

Fig. 6.11. Doodle Diagram for Drift Theory

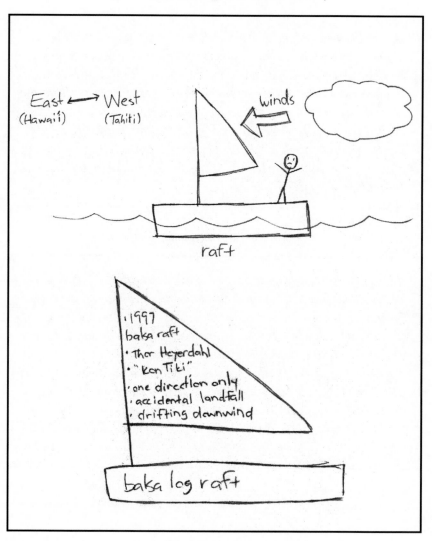

Fig. 6.10. Doodle Diagram for Intentional Voyaging

5. **Evaluate and discuss during a gallery walk.** Students can post their completed Doodle Diagrams around the classroom or on *Microsoft PowerPoint*® slides. In a gallery walk, other students visit the doodles and the artist comments on their content. In the case of the examples shown in figures 6.9 through 6.12, the crucial idea is that the 1980 voyage of the Hokulea double sailing canoe with navigator Nainoa Thompson managed to sail back to Tahiti from Hawaii, effectively countering the earlier Drift Theory that assumed Polynesian sailors wandered aimlessly across the Pacific, never to return to their departure point.

Reflections on 21st Century Learning

1. How do you currently address comprehension in your classroom?

2. Which of the comprehension strategies in this chapter would you like to incorporate in your teaching? Why?

3. How do you see these strategies assisting ELL students in your classroom?

4. How do you see these strategies impacting struggling readers?

Chapter 7

Strategies for Building Study Skills

Developing students' independent learning strategies is crucial for their future success in academic and career learning. Metacognitive strategies that help students monitor their comprehension and use fix-up strategies (like rereading and note-taking) are critical elements of reading print and online texts. The strategies described in this chapter are designed to help your students study challenging materials effectively:

- PLAE (Preplan, List, Activate, Evaluate)

- Verbatim Split Page Procedure

- I-Search Paper

- RAFT (Role, Audience, Format, Topic)

PLAE

Description

PLAE (*Preplan, List, Activate, and Evaluate*) provides students a guiding metacognitive strategy for studying (Simpson and Nist 1990).

Timing

- ☑ Pre-reading
- ☑ During Reading
- ☑ Post-reading

Logistics

- ○ Teacher preparation time
- ◐ Instructional time
- ○ Complexity

Targets

- ☐ Increase fluency
- ☑ Increase attention during reading
- ☑ Utilize prior knowledge to facilitate comprehension
- ☐ Expand or restructure knowledge
- ☑ Enhance learning and memory

PLAE Directions

1. **Preplan.** Help students set an overall plan on how to study the material. This may entail asking such questions as:

   - Should I summarize, take notes, or reread?
   - What kind of a test is the instructor going to give?
   - Do I want to study by myself or in a small group?

2. **List.** Have students answer the questions they generate. This activity should result in planned behaviors rather than thoughtless or reflexive ones. The planned behaviors should be written down. For example: *I will read this chapter twice. I will ask my teacher whether the test will be essay or multiple-choice. I will ask Juan and Beth if they want to study with me tomorrow.*

3. **Activate.** This is a monitoring behavior. Basically, students need to regularly ask themselves, *Am I following my plan?* as they move through the material.

4. **Evaluate.** This is a feedback step as students assess whether or not the plan has worked for them. For example: *Was it worth studying with Juan and Beth? Would I do it again?*

PLAE is deceptively simple, so much so that you may be tempted to dismiss it as superfluous. Yet, we believe that a strategy as simple as this is fundamental and not at all too obvious to bother with as you are teaching. How many times have you arrived at school only to discover that you had forgotten your lunch, house keys, wallet, purse, or other important item? If the average adult simply stopped at the front door before leaving and asked, "Do I have everything I need to take with me?" it would probably save millions of dollars in gasoline and aspirin. So, plan on introducing the strategy to your students and guiding them through its initial use—students should be able to do PLAE independently after that.

Verbatim Split Page Procedure

Description

The *Verbatim Split Page Procedure* (VSPP) is a blend of various strategies for note-taking during the reading of assignments or can be adapted for note-taking during lectures. Unfortunately, writing in the text, the best method of responding while reading, is not an option for most middle and secondary students because the books belong to the school. The combined use of underlining main ideas, starring important items, asking and answering questions, and marking evaluative comments in the margins provide highly personal and convenient response modes during reading.

In the absence of this option, however, we must examine what we know about reading and taking notes and consider some alternative study strategies. We know that:

- Students need instruction in how to take notes; we cannot make the assumption that students will do so on their own.

- Students must be able to differentiate important material from supporting detail and irrelevant information before note-taking will succeed.

- In order for students to benefit from note-taking instruction, review is essential, particularly in delayed recall situations.

VSPP combines these functions about good note-taking, and we recommend it for use with middle and secondary students.

If students have access to laptop computers, SmartPhones, MP3 players, or other similar technology, they can create a VSPP template for note-taking using a digital form of storage.

Indeed, most SmartPhones have a note-taking function, as do MP3 players like the Apple iPod®. Notes can also be dictated into a SmartPhone or laptop via a simple microphone and stored in podcast form.

Timing	**Logistics**
☑ Pre-reading	○ Teacher preparation time
☑ During Reading	◑ Instructional time
☑ Post-reading	◑ Complexity

Targets

☐ Increase fluency

☑ Increase attention during reading

☐ Utilize prior knowledge to facilitate comprehension

☐ Expand or restructure knowledge

☑ Enhance learning and memory

Verbatim Split Page Procedure Directions

1. **Recording notes.** Begin teaching VSPP by having students divide their notebook paper so that 40 percent of each page lies to the left and 60 percent to the right. During *lectures*, instruct students to take notes only on the left-hand side. All notes should be verbatim and brief so that minimum amounts of mental energy are expended on writing so that full attention can be focused on listening to the lecture. During *reading*, the opposite is true. Notes should be taken from the text and written on the right-hand side.

2. **Organizing notes.** Nearly everyone has had the experience of taking abundant notes for a class only to find those notes either unreadable or bizarre when it came time to study for the exam. Therefore, it is necessary to reorganize notes in a form that is understandable for later study. After *lecture*, the right side of the notebook paper is used for reorganizing and expanding upon the scribbles to the left. Students should be encouraged to:

- place lecture information in an outline format;
- interpret notes and then encode them in their own words;
- expand notes to include lecture information that the student did not have time to note;
- write out whole words, phrases, and sentences so that notes will be clear in the future.

After *reading*, in the opposite manner, use the left side of the paper to jot down key words, abbreviations, and whatever clues are necessary to help students use these clipped notes as memory triggers for studying the actual notes on the right side of the paper. In either lecture or reading, the end result of note-taking should look like the example in figure 7.1 on the next page.

Fig. 7.1. Organizing Notes

Space Phenomena	Space Phenomena
Planets, stars, asteroids, comets, quasars—Planets are Merc., Ven., E, Mrs., Jup., Sat., Ur., Nep. Imp. info Merc. closest to sun Jup. biggest Sat. rings Mrs. most likely to have life—no Indic. so far	Planets in our solar system 1. Mercury is smallest, hottest, and closest to the sun 2. Jupiter is the biggest 3. Saturn has rings 4. Mars is the most likely to have life, but there are no indications of life so far.

3. **Studying notes.** The 40 percent clipped note column on the left serves as the basis for studying the notes. Students try to recall the expanded information using the clipped notes as a prompt. In addition to the split-page note-taking structure, teaching students to consciously self-monitor their note-taking before they begin and after they finish can improve their note-taking performance through more active processing of the material. Based on teacher modeling of the self-questioning routine, students should begin and end note-taking with these questions:

   • **Before note-taking:** *What is my purpose for note-taking? Am I interested in this topic and, if not, how will I increase interest and concentration?*

   • **After note-taking:** *Did I achieve my purpose? Did I maintain concentration and deal with comprehension failures?*

I-Search Paper

Description

The *I-Search Paper* is an alternative to the more traditional research paper. Unlike traditional research papers where there is a tendency for students to report on a topic by reading and distilling the works of others, in I-Search Papers students investigate a topic of their choosing by interviewing experts, visiting places, and telling the story of their search.

Timing

- ☑ Pre-reading
- ☑ During Reading
- ☑ Post-reading

Logistics

- ◑ Teacher preparation time
- ◑ Instructional time
- ● Complexity

Targets

- ☐ Increase fluency
- ☑ Increase attention during reading
- ☑ Utilize prior knowledge to facilitate comprehension
- ☑ Expand or restructure knowledge
- ☑ Enhance learning and memory

I-Search Paper Directions

1. **Choose a topic.** Students should select topics of personal interest. For example, Jennifer, a middle school student, had regularly visited the zoo for years. The pandas mystified her, and her I-Search Paper investigated how they are cared for in the city zoo. Another student, Fabio, wanted to find out more about how guitars are made. Both students used search engines to consult Internet sources that might add to their I-Search Papers.

2. **Carry out the search.** Share the topic with the class and see if anyone has some ideas about where to find an expert to interview. For example, Jennifer's interest in pandas put her in contact with the head veterinarian at the city zoo. Fabio's search sent him to a luthier, a person who makes stringed instruments. Before contacting and interviewing the veterinarian and luthier, these students did some background reading on their respective topics, including both library print resources and search advice by the media specialist at their school. From this background reading, they made some interview questions on their respective topics. Jennifer asked the veterinarian at the zoo why pandas are on the endangered species list. Fabio asked the luthier how much it costs to build a handmade koa guitar.

3. **Conduct the interview.** Using a digital recorder to retain the information they needed for the I-Search Paper, Jennifer and Fabio interviewed the experts they located. They were able to take short video clips of the experts they interviewed that included a clip of a panda and, in Fabio's case, clips of koa guitars. These were uploaded to YouTube™ as part of their I-Search papers, with the URL listed for the reader. They obtained recommendations for further reading into the topic from these experts. For example, the luthier told Fabio to read a specific book on guitar making.

4. **Write the paper.** Use the I-Search Paper experience as a way of telling the story of how the paper evolved. Anything important in the search process should be included, and the format can follow these four categories of information:

   a. **What did the student know when the topic was selected?** For example, Jennifer did not know that there are only about 1,000 pandas living in the mountains in China. The pandas depend heavily on the food source of their bamboo forests that are vulnerable to logging and a natural life and death cycle.

   b. **Why did the student decide to write on this topic?** In Jennifer's case, she worked as a volunteer at the zoo. She had a long-standing interest in biology and in becoming a veterinarian specializing in the care of large, endangered zoo animals. Fabio played an old koa guitar that once belonged to his grandfather, and he was interested in how it was made. He dreamed about someday making his own guitar.

   c. **Describe the search.** Fabio's paper described his visit to the luthier. Fabio commented on the old industrial warehouse where the luthier worked and how neat everything was. Fabio spent two afternoons at the guitar maker's workshop and read the recommended book on guitar making to add to the research on his paper.

   d. **What did the student learn?** Jennifer included information on the panda's diet in the zoo (e.g., bamboo, apples, carrots, sweet potatoes, pans of slurpy ice, and mixtures of milk, eggs, and ground vegetables), sleep habits (e.g., 12 to 14 hours per day), and reproduction. In addition, she learned that in China, breeding programs are used to raise pandas in captivity to be released into the wild.

The I-Search Paper should conclude with a list of sources, experts, and key people involved in supplying ideas and insights for the paper. The I-Search paper goes well with cooperative learning. For example, rather than using individual I-Search Paper topics, a small group or team of students can collaborate to investigate a topic about which they share a common interest. The I-Search Paper is also a good alternative to the traditional research paper for multicultural topics, English language learners, and struggling readers because of its experiential nature.

RAFT

Description

RAFT (Role, Audience, Format, Topic) is a writing activity that engages students in thinking deeply about a topic, thereby enhancing learning and retention of new information. Students select—or are assigned—a role, audience, format, and topic related to the reading assignment. From a reading assignment about nutrition, for example, a stick of butter (role) might be communicating with heart arteries (audience) by letter (format) about the importance of having health insurance (topic). The RAFT format encourages student responses that are highly creative and interesting. In addition, RAFT is a strategy that requires students to view reality from perspectives other than their own.

Timing
- ☐ Pre-reading
- ☐ During Reading
- ☑ Post-reading

Logistics
- ◐ Teacher preparation time
- ◐ Instructional time
- ● Complexity

Targets
- ☐ Increase fluency
- ☐ Increase attention during reading
- ☐ Utilize prior knowledge to facilitate comprehension
- ☑ Expand or restructure knowledge
- ☑ Enhance learning and memory

RAFT Directions

1. **Identify major concepts.** Evaluate the reading assignment to identify the major concepts that will be emphasized in the RAFT assignment.

2. **Complete the RAFT options.** Prepare the RAFT assignment by listing possible roles, audiences, formats, and topics (see figure 7.2 on page 151). In history or English, students can take on various roles (e.g., kings, serfs, horses) with a variety of audiences, including future generations or tourists. Formats can range across a wide array of possibilities, including multimedia, digital ads, letters, memos, video clips, diaries, pleas, travel brochures, advertisements, and so on. Advice columns, love letters, yearbook entries, and a multitude of other formats are also possible. RAFT provides a voice for those elements of history, biology, and other fields that often go unnoticed. For example, the sword used in a murder in a Shakespeare drama could speak through the vehicle of the writer, expressing its angst at being used against its will to murder a king. RAFT affords a highly creative exploration of topics from multiple perspectives (see figure 7.3 on page 152 for an example on Gettysburg).

3. **Introduce RAFT to the class.** RAFT is a complex writing assignment and will prove challenging for many students. It will be useful to provide the class with simple practice examples: for instance, a cow (role) writing a letter (format) to a fast food company (audience) about the importance of reducing saturated fat in the diet (topic).

4. **Create individual RAFT assignments.** There are at least four possibilities for creating individual RAFT assignments:

- Allow students to select their own roles, audiences, formats, and topics.
- Teacher selects a topic for students.
- Students select topics for each other
- Use dice or some other procedure to randomly assign roles, audiences, formats, and topics.

We suggest experimentation.

5. **Assessment.** Depending upon your purposes and the age and sophistication of your students, you may or may not want to grade the assignment. However, given the highly creative nature of RAFT, we recommend grading criteria and rubrics that are not overly dependent upon grammar and mechanics, especially if the writing is done in class and without the benefits of a dictionary. (See *RubiStar*, http://rubistar.4teachers.org/index.php, and other customizable rubric websites for templates you can use).

Fig. 7.2. Template for RAFT Assignments

RAFT

Name: _____   **Date:** _____

Directions: This is a writing assignment in which you will play the role of a person or thing from the reading assignment listed below. You will have to write to an audience that may be a single person or a group. The topic of your writing will also be based on the reading assignment. Finally, your writing will be in a particular format, such as a letter or newspaper article. The minimum and maximum length of your writing, due date/time, and grading criteria are described below.

Reading Assignment: _____

Main Topic: _____

Role	Audience	Format	Topic
_____	_____	_____	_____
_____	_____	_____	_____
_____	_____	_____	_____
_____	_____	_____	_____
_____	_____	_____	_____

Minimum Length: _____

Maximum Length: _____

Due date/Time: _____

Grading criteria: _____

Baldwin, Readence, and Bean 2004

Figure 7.3. RAFT Assignment for Battle of Gettysburg

RAFT

Name: _____   **Date:** _____

Directions: This is a writing assignment in which you will play the role of a person or thing from the reading assignment listed below. You will have to write to an audience that may be a single person or a group. The topic of your writing will also be based on the reading assignment. Finally, your writing will be in a particular format, such as a letter or newspaper article. The minimum and maximum length of your writing, due date/time, and grading criteria are described below.

Reading Assignment: _Assignment Chapter 23, pp. 166–174_

Main Topic: _Civil War Battle of Gettysburg_

Role	Audience	Format	Topic
Confederate Private	Abraham Lincoln	Newspaper Article	Slavery
General Pickett	Mother of Dead Soldier	Diary Entry	States' Rights
A cannon	Bayonet	Letter	Freedom
Union Surgeon	Newspaper Editor in 1859	Encyclopedia Entry	Death
Traveler	Squirrel on Little Roundtop	Advertisement	Honor

Minimum Length: _____

Maximum Length: _____

Due date/Time: _____

Grading criteria: _____

Baldwin, Readence, and Bean 2004

Reflections on 21st Century Learning

1. How do you currently develop students' independent study approaches in your classroom?

2. Which of the study strategies in this chapter would you like to incorporate in your teaching? Why?

3. What role does writing serve as an independent study approach in your classroom?

4. How will you differentiate instruction for students who need more guidance in using study strategies?

Strategies for Developing Critical Reading

Without a doubt, critical reading is an essential skill to have in the 21st century. As you develop your students' awareness of misinformation and flaws in text arguments, you are helping them to become astute citizens who are capable of deconstructing and critiquing ideas. The strategies described in this chapter are designed to scaffold the critical reading process in ways that engage students in dissecting and evaluating ideas:

- Polar Opposites

- Opinion-Proof

- REAP (Read, Encode, Annotate, Ponder)

- Phony Document Strategy

Polar Opposites

Description

Polar Opposites is a strategy that provides an excellent foundation for critical reflection and discussion (Bean and Bishop 1992; Bean 2010). A rating scale gauges how students view a concept or idea. A Polar Opposites guide consists of descriptive adjectives such as *happy* versus *sad* that are supported or challenged by events in the text. Students can critically evaluate events in a story or expository selection, and even the most reticent students have a foundation for engaging in discussion and writing activities. In order to defend or refute a particular rating, students must return to the text for support. Thus, the strategy encourages critical reading.

Timing
- ☐ Pre-reading
- ☐ During Reading
- ☑ Post-reading

Logistics
- ◑ Teacher preparation time
- ◑ Instructional time
- ◑ Complexity

Targets
- ☐ Increase fluency
- ☐ Increase attention during reading
- ☐ Utilize prior knowledge to facilitate comprehension
- ☑ Expand or restructure knowledge
- ☑ Enhance learning and memory

Polar Opposites Directions

1. **Prepare the guide.** Prepare four or five opposing statements or adjectives and their accompanying antonyms. Evaluate the reading assignment to identify candidates for Polar Opposites. Usually, these will be traits or viewpoints that are subject to variation in personal perceptions.

2. **Introduce the activity.** Explain to students the concept of *polarity* (opposites and antonyms) and the fact that individuals may have very different perceptions of the same event or circumstance. As an example, place the following Polar Opposite on the board, and ask students to copy it and place a check mark on the line that comes closest to their perception of the current level of temperature comfort in the classroom:

hot _____ _____ _____ _____ _____ cold

   A check mark on the various lines would correspond to—from left to right—hot, warm, neutral, cool, and cold, respectively. Provide additional examples until students are comfortable with completing Polar Opposites. Then have the students complete the exercise.

3. **Defend the ratings.** Students should be prepared to defend their ratings and perceptions in small-group discussions or as a writing activity. For example, in John Grisham's novel, *The King of Torts* (2003), the main character Clay Carter, a public defender attorney, becomes wealthy overnight in mass torts against pharmaceutical companies. The Polar Opposites guide for that novel follows in figure 8.1 on the following page.

Fig. 8.1 Polar Opposites Guide for *The King of Torts*

Directions: For each polar opposite, place a check mark on the line which best describes Clay Carter in the first two chapters of the book:

ethical ＿＿＿ ＿＿＿ ＿＿＿ ＿＿＿ ＿＿＿ unethical

self-critical ＿＿＿ ＿＿＿ ＿＿＿ ＿＿＿ ＿＿＿ self-absorbed

compassionate ＿＿＿ ＿＿＿ ＿＿＿ ＿＿＿ ＿＿＿ callous

lower class ＿＿＿ ＿＿＿ ＿＿＿ ＿＿＿ ＿＿＿ wealthy

Opinion-Proof

Description

Opinion-Proof is a strategy that guides students in the evaluation of arguments supporting an opinion (Santa, Dailey, and Nelson 1985). Students must form an opinion, support the opinion, search for any fallacies in their reasoning, and write persuasively about the opinion.

Timing	**Logistics**
☐ Pre-reading	○ Teacher preparation time
☐ During Reading	◑ Instructional time
☑ Post-reading	● Complexity

Targets

☐ Increase fluency

☐ Increase attention during reading

☐ Utilize prior knowledge to facilitate comprehension

☑ Expand or restructure knowledge

☐ Enhance learning and memory

Opinion-Proof Directions

Start by modeling the opinion-proof process. It is important to illustrate the characteristics of an opinion statement. In addition, students can generate and exchange their own opinion statement examples. These steps are helpful in creating effective opinion-proof strategy lessons:

1. **Discuss opinion statements with the students.** An opinion is a conclusion that is subject to dispute and is difficult to prove or disprove. Opinion statements frequently include conditional verbs such as *could, would, should,* and *might* or comparative adjectives such as *best, happiest,* or *slower.* Opinion statements are often difficult or impossible to prove. It is important to note that opinions are not the same as inaccurate statements of fact. To say, for example, that the first president of the United States was John F. Kennedy is simply an inaccurate statement that is easily disproved. On the other hand, the claim that Kennedy was the best president or the worst president would be subject to endless dispute and is, therefore, an opinion.

2. **Create an opinion statement.** Write the opinion statement or have students write one. For example, in a senior high school economics class, students considered the concept of scarcity and its relationship to economic choices. Because their school district was under intense budget pressure, classes in art, music, and physical education were going to be reduced or eliminated in the next year's curriculum. The students had to evaluate this opinion statement:

    > *Opinion statement:* The elimination of art, music, and physical education will limit students' career opportunities in the future.

3. **Define opinions.** Discuss with students the concept that sound opinions have evidence to support them, and that the amount and quality of the evidence is crucial in making a judgment about the validity of the opinion. In the economics example, students might get on the Internet and research articles arguing for the importance of the arts in problem-solving and the value of exercise in learning.

4. **Examine the evidence.** Have students share evidence on the value of the arts and physical education on an overhead, *Microsoft PowerPoint*®, or whiteboard presentation.

5. **Create the essay.** Write an essay as a group or have students develop independent essays using the opinion and the evidence they discovered in their research.

6. **Evaluate the essay.** Have students evaluate the persuasiveness of their essays, searching for reasoning fallacies. A rubric might be created to judge the essays. Also, the list of fallacies (figure 8.2 on the following page) should be helpful in evaluating arguments.

In our continuing example of the economics class, students debated the opinion about the curriculum cuts using the concept of scarcity. *Scarcity*, within economic theory, is a condition where our wants are greater than the available resources to satisfy them. If the choice of what subjects or classes to offer entails making judgment calls about core versus non-core subject areas, the decision to maintain essential subjects in mathematics, science, English, and history may be the one that is preferable. Indeed, students were hard pressed to find evidence supporting the opinion that their futures would be limited by budget cuts in non-core subject areas. This opinion suffered from the common fallacies of false cause and hasty generalization. Counter evidence from graduates of technical magnet schools and other alternative educational approaches needed to be considered. Nevertheless, this opinion statement went to the heart of scarcity of resources and economic choices.

Fig. 8.2 Reasoning Fallacies

1. **Authority**—treating authority as the last word

2. **Emotion**—treating emotion as proof

3. **Force**—using threats to support the validity of a claim

4. **People**—supporting a claim because it is popular

5. **Ignorance**—arguing that a claim is correct because the opposite cannot be proven

6. **Begging the Question**—a claim with arguments that do not support it

7. **Contradiction**—sharing information that contradicts a claim

8. **Evading the Issue**—talking around the issue

9. **False Analogy**—comparing unmatched things

10. **False Cause**—linking an effect to a cause without evidence

11. **Hasty Generalization**—leaping to a conclusion without adequate examples

12. **Poisoning the Well**—getting stuck in one position and viewing everything in light of that position

REAP

Description

REAP (*Read, Encode, Annotate, Ponder*) is a critical reading strategy that engages students in writing annotations to evaluate the message and underlying motives in a text. REAP involves:

- **R:** Reading the passage
- **E:** Encoding the message by translating the passage into their own words
- **A:** Annotating or writing the translated passage summary in their notes
- **P:** Pondering the message to judge the underlying motives driving an author to convey a message (Eanet and Manzo 1976).

A good annotation first states the author's thesis and then offers an opinion about that thesis. The Internet, allows for sharing annotations by archiving them for others.

Timing	Logistics
☐ Pre-reading	◖ Teacher preparation time
☐ During Reading	◖ Instructional time
☑ Post-reading	● Complexity

Targets

- ☐ Increase fluency
- ☐ Increase attention during reading
- ☐ Utilize prior knowledge to facilitate comprehension
- ☑ Expand or restructure knowledge
- ☑ Enhance learning and memory

REAP Directions

1. **Select a passage.** Your selected passage should have some underlying motive in its message (e.g., to get the reader to purchase a product or buy into a particular viewpoint). Model the four types of REAP annotations (found in step 4) before students begin using the strategy independently. (The example in figure 8.2 illustrates this process with a passage aimed at selling a new speed reading program to student consumers.)

2. **R (Read):** Have students read the selection.

Fig. 8.2. Model of the REAP Annotations

The *Auditory Speed Reading Program* Promotional Message

Do you spend too many hours trying to read your homework assignments? The Auditory Speed Reading Program can help. You can use this program and its software to scan any passage into your computer (scanner not included). Once on your computer, the microphone and software prompts you to read faster if your reading rate drops below the preferred study rate of 300 words-per-minute. Much like a warning device on a car that beeps if you exceed the speed limit, the Auditory Speed Reading Program offers an array of irritating voices to get your reading speed in gear. These range from a Marine Corps drill instructor's voice prompting you to "hurry up" if you slow down too much, to various beeps and other sounds to get you moving at top speed. You will finish your homework in no time at all, guaranteed.

---

3. **E (Encode):** Instruct students to write a brief summary of the selection:

The article consists of ad copy for a special speed-reading software package that students can install on their computers to help them pace any readings they scan in. The ad says that the speed-reading program works by prompting the reader if he or she slows down too much in their oral reading of the passage. The program works by using pre-selected voices or sounds that are "irritating" enough to get the reader to accelerate his or her pace.

4. **A (Annotate):** Have students write annotations on note cards or sticky notes and share their ideas in small groups. Various forms of annotations can be explored including:

- **Summary Annotations**

  The Auditory Speed Reading Program prompts the reader to move ahead using pre-programmed voices and sounds the reader can select.

- **Thesis Annotations**

  The Auditory Speed Reading Program is designed to help students complete their homework faster.

- **Critical Annotations**

  The Auditory Speed Reading Program has a number of problems. These include a reliance on oral versus silent reading, distracting sounds, and no evidence that it helps comprehension.

- **Question Annotations**

  Are there other speed-reading programs that might actually help a reader's comprehension? How do they work?

5. **P (Ponder):** Instruct students to use their annotations to evaluate the content and presentation of the information, points of view, and purpose of the selection:

> *There are a number of problems with this ad. First, it assumes students read study material orally, which is rarely the case. Silent reading is the usual mode. Second, the "irritating" sounds would likely disrupt concentration, reducing comprehension of study material in the process. Most students prefer not to be interrupted when they are tackling difficult texts. Finally, this ad seems to support a program that, while it guarantees fast completion of homework, offers little in the way of assurances about comprehension. The ad writer's motive here is to sell this software to consumers, regardless of its real value.*

Phony Document Strategy

Description

The *Phony Document Strategy* engages students in a critical evaluation of text that is essentially false. The Phony Document Strategy is based on a teacher-authored letter, or other text (e.g., an advertisement) that purports to be authentic (Vanderhoof et al. 1992). While the text reads as a perfectly plausible account of a key aspect of a novel, historical event, or scientific experiment, it is completely fictitious. Students must engage in a close, critical reading of the document to ferret out the embedded errors. The teacher creates the document and, initially, supports its authenticity.

Timing
- ☐ Pre-reading
- ☐ During Reading
- ☑ Post-reading

Logistics
- ● Teacher preparation time
- ● Instructional time
- ● Complexity

Targets
- ☐ Increase fluency
- ☐ Increase attention during reading
- ☐ Utilize prior knowledge to facilitate comprehension
- ☑ Expand or restructure knowledge
- ☐ Enhance learning and memory

Phony Document Strategy Directions

1. **Create the document.** Create a phony, but plausibly written document such as a letter, a critique, or a news article.

2. **Evaluate the document.** Ask students to read and judge the accuracy of the document and its value as something that could be purchased. They must engage in a close reading, checking the authority of the purported author, dates, assertions, places, and so on with other sources.

3. **Engage in discussion.** Conduct small-group and whole-class discussions about the document's accuracy and value *after* students have completed their individual evaluations.

The phony news article in figure 8.3 on the following page reports on a flawless new breed of dog that has been scientifically altered through cloning to avoid many of the health problems that plague most purebred dog breeds. This article would accompany text readings and concept building in biology concerning cloning.

Fig. 8.3. News Article for Phony Document

New Dog Breed Avoids Health Pitfalls

Many purebred dogs and their owners unfortunately fall victim to unscrupulous breeding practices. Hip dysplasia and a host of other well-known ailments eventually take their toll on unwary dog owners and their pets. The cost of treatments can be astronomical. For example, replacing a dog's hips can easily run in the thousands of dollars. Fortunately, a team of scientists at the Canine Genetics Center at the University of the Desert has, through cloning, devised a new dog breed, affectionately called the Wolfe Dog. The name acknowledges the Wolfe Foundation, the underwriter of this canine genome research. Wolfe Dog combines the best traits of mongrels that typically have few, if any ailments. Wolfe Dogs are the result of cloning the hardiest mongrel dogs from around the world. They are medium-sized, somewhat intelligent, and devoid of all the problems normally associated with high-strung purebreds. But there is a downside to their development. If you want to be the proud owner of one of the early prototypes of the Wolfe Dog, you must be willing to shell out over $10,000. And, they cannot be entered in sanctioned Kennel Club events because there is, as yet, no certification for this new breed. Nevertheless, you will undoubtedly be very pleased to be the proud owner of the first Wolfe Dog on your block. To find out more about this new breed of dog, you can visit the Wolfe Dog research website at: *http://www.WolfeDog.com*.

The discussion of this document should revolve around the many obvious flaws. Cloning animals is highly controlled and controversial. The end result of such experiments, in this case the mythical Teflon Dog, would not be for sale, and it is hard to imagine anyone paying $10,000 for one. There is no Milk Bone Center, nor a university called University of the Desert. Students can engage in a close reading of phony documents you develop to question and critique underlying assumptions, facts, figures, and unusual claims or warrants. While it takes time to create phony documents, the process of scrutinizing them is worth every minute. Students develop a healthy skepticism as a result of this strategy.

Reflections on 21st Century Learning

1. Why is critical reading important for your students?

2. Which critical reading strategy would you like to incorporate in your classroom? Why?

3. How will you differentiate instruction in critical reading for students who need more guidance in this process?

Strategies for Enhancing Fluency

Reading demanding content-area texts in print and online takes a significant amount of attention. Indeed, if your students get bogged down in word-by-word reading and decoding, comprehension is nearly impossible. Developing students' fluency through the strategies described in this chapter can go a long way towards ensuring that students overcome the pitfalls of word-by-word reading:

- Choral Reading

- Sustained Silent Reading

- Radio Reading

Choral Reading

Description

Non-fluent readers are easy to recognize. They read slowly, haltingly, and with poor intonation, and their reading comprehension is minimal. They may be able to pronounce most of the words they encounter, but it is clear that they have not yet developed an autopilot for reading. For those who are non-fluent, reading is no fun at all. It is possible for individuals within a group to sing a song, recite a poem, or complete the Pledge of Allegiance when it would be difficult or impossible for them to do these tasks alone. Similarly, *Choral Reading* is a group strategy that gives less fluent readers the opportunity to use verbal cues from more fluent readers during reading (McCauley and McCauley 1992). It permits them to decode words more rapidly, to read faster, and to use more natural intonation, all of which should help non-fluent readers increase fluency and develop an autopilot.

Timing
- ☐ Pre-reading
- ☑ During Reading
- ☐ Post-reading

Logistics
- ○ Teacher preparation time
- ○ Instructional time
- ○ Complexity

Targets
- ☑ Increase fluency
- ☐ Increase attention during reading
- ☐ Utilize prior knowledge to facilitate comprehension
- ☐ Expand or restructure knowledge
- ☐ Enhance learning and memory

Choral Reading Directions

1. **Determine instructional readiness.** Explain to students that reading is a lot like singing, that it can be fun and that having a good time with reading is the objective of the exercise. Students, especially those who are non-fluent, will be more likely to participate if they see choral reading as a pleasurable activity.

2. **Select the text.** Pick an interesting and relatively easy text. If students enjoy a particular selection, you may want to use it repeatedly. The objective in choral reading is to get all students—including non-fluent readers who hate reading—to participate in the activity. Comprehension and learning are secondary considerations in choral reading.

3. **Assign students to groups.** It is possible to have an entire class engage in simultaneous choral reading. However, 30 or 40 adolescent voices can be loud, and it is difficult to monitor what the non-fluent readers are doing. Are they following the text or just moving their lips? An alternative is to assign students to groups of four to eight. Each group should have several fluent readers so that non-fluent readers have appropriate models.

4. **Read the selection.** Groups can take turns reading for about one minute at a time. Choral reading should only take five to ten minutes of class time. You should participate to enhance the modeling of good reading behaviors. If you are brave, you can try syncopated choral reading with all groups participating at the same time, but with each group starting a few words or a sentence apart. This is simply a variation of "Row, Row, Row Your Boat" and can be used to increase selective attention or the difficulty of the activity.

5. **Evaluate the strategy.** Avoid formal evaluation. Consider the activity a success if you get universal participation and smiles.

Sustained Silent Reading

Description

Sustained Silent Reading (SSR) is a systematic program that establishes regular reading times for students. Its fundamental objective is to provide students with an opportunity to develop their reading fluency by practicing their reading skills using pleasurable content-related materials. SSR has a positive impact on students' attitudes toward reading and their long-term interest in reading for pleasure.

Timing

- ☐ Pre-reading
- ☑ During Reading
- ☐ Post-reading

Logistics

- ○ Teacher preparation time
- ◑ Instructional time
- ○ Complexity

Targets

- ☑ Increase fluency
- ☐ Increase attention during reading
- ☐ Utilize prior knowledge to facilitate comprehension
- ☐ Expand or restructure knowledge
- ☐ Enhance learning and memory

Sustained Silent Reading Directions

1. **Determine Instructional readiness.** Discuss SSR with students. Let them know how the activity will be carried out and why they are doing it. Emphasize that SSR is supposed to be a pleasurable activity. Assure students that they will not be graded or asked questions about what they read. Since the stated purpose of SSR is to provide pleasurable practice in reading to increase fluency, students should be informed that certain types of materials are inappropriate. Textbooks, magazines, comics, and newspapers should not be used. Textbooks are seldom selected for pleasure reading, and comics, magazines, and newspapers lend themselves to picture-looking rather than reading. If you plan to use SSR to further expand students' understanding of events in history, science, or mathematics units, then you will need a well-stocked collection of young adult novels from which students can select. Your guidance in this area will be crucial, as students often have no idea which books match their interests within a content area like science or history. Knowing students' interests and being familiar with juvenile and adolescent literature related to your field are important preparatory steps before launching into SSR.

2. **Begin the reading activity.** Once you have completed the instructional readiness stage, use the following guidelines to engage students in Sustained Silent Reading:

    *   Everyone must read, and this includes the teacher. SSR is not a mini-study period for students, and it is not a break or prep period for teachers. Doing homework, getting coffee, grading papers, and other extraneous activities are put aside to allow time for reading. It is essential that the teacher *model* SSR by reading right along with students.

- SSR should be uninterrupted. Let students know that they are not to sharpen pencils, gossip, or ask questions like, *What does this word mean?* In addition, colleagues should know that they are not to disturb a class during SSR. It may be worthwhile to hang a sign on the door: *SSR in progress. Do not disturb!* It is difficult to increase reading fluency with interruptions.

- SSR should occur on a regularly scheduled basis, as often as it is realistically possible in your classroom. Time limits for SSR should vary according to the age and general maturity of the class. We recommend beginning with five minutes and then gradually increasing the time as students adjust to the routine and develop a capacity to attend to reading for more than brief periods of time. Be careful not to increase the time too quickly, perhaps a minute every week or two. Each teacher should judge the amount of time to be allocated to SSR based upon student abilities and curricular demands. The benefits that can be gained from reading will enrich your instruction, particularly if students are reading material related to the topic under discussion.

- Time SSR with care. Use a kitchen timer placed on your desk, facing away from the students so they will not stare at it. Wall clocks make bad timing devices, as some students become clock watchers. Avoid using your wristwatch, since that encourages students to ask you about time remaining. Simply tell them that the kitchen timer will always indicate when SSR is over for the day.

- Avoid doing SSR immediately prior to tests since it will be difficult for students to concentrate knowing that a quiz or test is imminent. On test days, shift SSR to some later part of the class period or postpone it until the next day.

- Have effective strategies in place for keeping students on task and engaged. Off-task behavior can be handled in the following manner. You may have some students whose aversion to reading is so profound that they will refuse, initially, to participate in SSR. The very idea of reading for fun will be totally foreign to some students. Do not pressure them. You can force people to do something, but you cannot make them like it. Let problem students "sleep," just as long as they do not bother the group. As these students see others enjoying SSR, they will come to find reading preferable to inactivity. Let the class know that intentional disruption will result in termination of SSR for the day. If a student does something that causes half the class to stop reading, simply say: "I am sorry, but our SSR is over for today. Put your books away and begin _____." Move right along to the next scheduled activity without acknowledging the culprits or their actions. Because SSR is inherently pleasurable, peer pressure should serve to reduce individual disruptions.

Radio Reading

Description

Radio Reading derives its name from the analogy between a radio announcer's talking to a listening audience and an oral reading situation (Searfoss 1975). The reader functions as the radio announcer with a script, and the listeners serve as the audience listening to and thinking about a radio program. The reader's purpose is to communicate fluently and accurately a message through oral reading. The listeners respond by discussing and restating the message and evaluating whether the passage was clearly rendered. Radio Reading does not allow for prompting or correction; rather, it focuses instruction on the goal of communicating a message through fluent, accurate reading. The strategy may be conducted with the whole class or in small groups.

Timing
- ☐ Pre-reading
- ☑ During Reading
- ☐ Post-reading

Logistics
- ○ Teacher preparation time
- ◑ Instructional time
- ○ Complexity

Targets
- ☑ Increase fluency
- ☑ Increase attention during reading
- ☐ Utilize prior knowledge to facilitate comprehension
- ☐ Expand or restructure knowledge
- ☐ Enhance learning and memory

Radio Reading Directions

1. **Get started.** Discuss Radio Reading with students. The ground rules are simple: the reader reads and the listeners listen. Since the listeners will not have a copy of the material, close listening is emphasized. The teacher must also select material that is appropriate in difficulty and length. The material may be challenging, but not frustrating, and can be narrative or informational in content. As an alternative to teacher-selected material, and depending on the availability of computer equipment, the appropriate platform, and the sophistication of the students, students might create a podcast reading text aloud after rehearsing the piece. For example, the selection could be read into a mic using GarageBand™ and stored on iTunes®. Another alternative is having students read aloud and creating a short YouTube™ clip.

2. **Communicate the message.** Since the job of the reader is to convey a clear message, the reader is permitted to change words, insert new words, or omit words where warranted. The role of the reader is to read in a natural, speech-like manner with clearly articulated words and good intonation. If possible, radio readers should have an opportunity to read their scripts silently before being asked to perform. However, the reader is responsible for deciding when help is needed with an unknown word. When this happens, the reader is instructed to simply ask: *What is that word?* Since radio reading is based on fluency and communicating meaning, the reader should be given the word immediately and without any prompting so that there is as little interruption as possible.

3. **Check for understanding.** In Radio Reading, it is the listeners rather than the reader whose comprehension is assessed. Depending upon the teacher's preferences, the listeners may be asked to respond to text explicit, text implicit, and experience-based questions generated by the teacher, or listeners may be asked to summarize the text. The listeners may ask for a rereading if the message is not clearly understood. Once the meaning of the message is confirmed, the reader may continue or, in a small group situation, the role of the radio reader may rotate to give others the opportunity to read. Failure to broadcast a clear message after rereading will also cause the listeners to tune in a new station, that is, the reader's right to continue reading ceases, and a new radio reader takes over. The emphasis is always on communicating a fluent message.

Reflections on 21st Century Learning

1. Why is reading fluency important for your students?

2. Which reading fluency strategy would you like to incorporate in your classroom? Why?

3. How will you differentiate instruction in reading fluency for students who need more guidance in this process?

Strategies for Enhancing Online Reading Comprehension

Online reading material confronts your students with a boundless source of information that is at once a great resource and a potential source of difficulty, particularly for struggling readers. The potential for students to retrieve and believe misinformation on the Internet is high. The strategies described in this chapter are designed to help your students actively search for information and carefully consider the credibility of the sources they encounter in their online reading.

- SAND (Search, Analyze, Note Details)
- ISSDAT (Internet Search, Slow Down, and Think)

SAND

Description

SAND (Search, Analyze, Note Details) is a strategy that helps students avoid retrieving misinformation from the vast labyrinth of the Internet when they are searching for information on a topic. A methodical approach to searching the Internet and noting the credibility of various sites is preferable to randomly wandering into sites of little value or credibility. This strategy is particularly useful for history and science topics.

Timing
- ☐ Pre-reading
- ☑ During Reading
- ☑ Post-reading

Logistics
- ◑ Teacher preparation time
- ◑ Instructional time
- ◑ Complexity

Targets
- ☐ Increase fluency
- ☐ Increase attention during reading
- ☑ Utilize prior knowledge to facilitate comprehension
- ☑ Expand or restructure knowledge
- ☑ Enhance learning and memory

SAND Directions

Using SAND involves searching for information on the Internet while following a three-step process aimed at carefully evaluating website information:

1. **Search.** The student types a topic keyword or phrase (e.g., Oil Spill Causes) into the preferred search engine (Google™, Bing™, or others).

2. **Analyze.** The student analyzes the credibility and applicability of a site for his or her topic. For example, is it a site that is advertising a particular product for sale rather than offering objective information? Is it a site trying to persuade readers to believe something that may be erroneous?

3. **Note details.** Who created this site? Is it credible? (e.g., check the source and the credentials of the author). The student bookmarks sites that are worthwhile for the topic so they can backtrack and revisit them.

An example of a student's use of the SAND strategy is described in figure 10.1 on the following page.

Fig. 10.1. SAND Example

Researching Jesse James

Students in an American History class selected famous outlaws to research. This example traces a student's use of the SAND strategy to research and write a short biography chronicling the life and crimes of the outlaw Jesse James. Using the SAND strategy, this student, a struggling reader, was able to avoid some of the potential pitfalls that confront students while exploring the maze of the Internet with various search engines.

1. **Search.** The student types *Jesse James* into his Google™ search engine. Over six pages of sites come up in the search results.

2. **Analyze.** While some sites clearly relate to Jesse James the outlaw, many advertise biker Jesse James's West Coast Choppers shop and scream "Buy Stuff" to entice viewers to purchase tee-shirts and other merchandise. As seductive as these sites are to the student, he focuses on the history sites and avoids many of the sites ending in *.com* where items are offered for sale.

3. **Note Details.** The student identifies credible sites based on his teacher's modeling those of the Smithsonian, Annenberg, and other reputable history websites. He then has enough resource material to begin constructing a biography of Jesse James the outlaw, as opposed to Jesse James the contemporary biker.

ISSDaT

Description

ISSDaT (Internet Search, Slow Down, and Think) is a strategy that helps students make intertextual connections across diverse websites when searching for a topic to be developed into a media presentation, paper, or project (Bean 2010). The disparate nature of sites on the Internet presents a challenge to weaving together information on a topic.

Timing

- ☐ Pre-reading
- ☑ During Reading
- ☑ Post-reading

Logistics

- ◑ Teacher preparation time
- ◑ Instructional time
- ◑ Complexity

Targets

- ☐ Increase fluency
- ☐ Increase attention during reading
- ☑ Utilize prior knowledge to facilitate comprehension
- ☑ Expand or restructure knowledge
- ☑ Enhance learning and memory

ISSDaT Directions

Before asking students to use ISSDaT, do a think aloud to model the process for students.

1. **Internet search.** Type your topic keyword or phrase (e.g., *plants of the sonoran desert*) into your preferred search engine (Google™, Bing™) or others.

2. **Slow down.** Record and bookmark the URL so you can backtrack to it later. Evaluate the credibility of the site for your topic as you did with SAND.

3. **and Think.** Think about how each site relates to the others you have found in terms of weaving information from them into a coherent *Microsoft PowerPoint*® or project presentation.

A student's use of the ISSDaT strategy is illustrated in figure 10.2 on the following page.

Fig. 10.2. ISSDaT Example

Researching Puppy Mills

Students in a science class selected significant contemporary problems to research, like spaying and neutering pets and puppy mills. This example illustrates a student's use of the ISSDaT strategy to research and create a multimedia presentation about puppy mills.

Using the ISSDaT strategy, this student, an average reader, was able to identify key sites and begin thinking about how to weave them into a coherent multimedia presentation.

1. **Internet Search.** The student types "puppy mills" into her search engine. A number of URLs come up in the search results.

2. **Slow down.** She records and bookmarks various URLs from the Humane Society, ASPCA, and a site offering "Frequently Asked Questions" to help organize her presentation. She evaluates the credibility of the sites and includes some counterpoint sites that argue, from an owner's perspective, how wonderful puppy mill dogs can be. She also finds some YouTube™ video clips that will be helpful.

3. **and Think.** She thinks about how each site relates to the others and decides to create her presentation around myths and facts about puppy mills.

Reflections on 21st Century Learning

1. In what ways is searching the Internet different from reading print texts?

2. Which online reading comprehension strategy would you like to try in your classroom? Why?

3. Several online sources are listed in Appendix E. Which recommended website would you like to explore further? How would you incorporate the ideas from that website into your instruction?

Chapter Self-Tests

Chapter 1 Self-Test

Matching

Match the definition with the appropriate term.

Terms	Definitions
1. Content-area reading	**A.** The various skills and behaviors commonly associated with the teaching of reading in the primary grades.
2. Learning to read	**B.** The process of using reading to learn subject-matter concepts.
3. Reading to learn	**C.** The expertise necessary to comprehend and react to appropriate instructional materials in a given subject area.

Multiple-Choice Questions

Circle the letter of the best option.

1. Which of the following may present some difficulty in reading text material?

I. Vocabulary
II. Lack of background knowledge
III. Long, complicated sentences
IV. Explicit instruction

    A. I only

    B. I, II, and III only

    C. II and IV only

    D. I, II, III, and IV

2. Which of the following is *not* an advantage a teacher has over textbooks?

    A. activating prior knowledge

    B. focusing attention

    C. tailoring the message

    D. decoding unknown words

    E. monitoring comprehension

Performance Question

Explain the role of middle and secondary teachers in helping their students learn with texts.

Chapter 2 Self-Test

Matching

Match the definition with the appropriate term.

Terms

1. fonts
2. fixations
3. sight vocabulary
4. pursuit eye movements
5. saccadic eye movements
6. regressions
7. fluency
8. phonemic awareness
9. letter recognition
10. ligatures
11. phonics
12. word recognition
13. return sweeps
14. decoding
15. the correct pronunciation of *ghoti*

Definitions

A. The action of the eyes when moving from one fixed object to another.

B. The ability to distinguish one speech sound from another.

C. The ability to see a written word and say it.

D. The action of the eyes when moving backwards on a line of print.

E. Written words recognized instantly and without effort.

F. Pronounced *fish*, the *gh* in *enough*, the *o* in *women*, and the *ti* in *ignition*.

G. The various styles of printed and written letters.

H. The eyes moving from the end of one line of print to the beginning of the next.

I. The conversion of written text to spoken language equivalents.

J. The action of the eyes when following a moving target.

K. Fast, accurate, and effortless decoding.

L. The ability to distinguish one letter from another.

M. The little lines or strokes that connect written letters.

N. A set of rules for associating sounds with letters.

O. The window of information when the eyes are at rest on a line of print.

Multiple-Choice Questions

Circle the letter of the best option.

1. Which of the following problems is a fluent reader most likely to have?

    A. poor word recognition

    B. lack of attention in comprehension

    C. inefficient eye movements

    D. a cheap cell phone

2. Which of the following is not required for decoding text?

    A. pursuit eye movements

    B. phonemic awareness

    C. letter recognition

    D. phonics

3. Reading a text with an unusual font might result in all of the following except:

    A. reduced comprehension

    B. faster reading rate

    C. fixations of greater duration

    D. increased attention to decoding

Performance Question

Speed reading franchises typically claim that adults can learn to read thousands of words per minute. Based on the information about the reading process presented in this chapter, is speed reading possible?

Chapter 3 Self-Test

Matching

Match the definition with the appropriate term.

Terms

1. on your own

2. selective attention

3. right on the page

4. reading autopilot

5. think-and-search

6. prior knowledge

7. metacognition

Definitions

A. the ability to screen out unwanted sensory information

B. text explicit comprehension

C. text implicit comprehension

D. an organized store of information based on a person's cumulative experiences

E. relieves the reader of any need to attend to decoding processes

F. awareness of one's own mental processes

G. experience-based comprehension

Multiple-Choice Questions

Circle the letter of the best option.

1. Building students' content vocabulary knowledge is important for reading to learn because it:

   A. makes them more eloquent.

   B. helps them get through assignments quickly.

   C. reduces reliance on asking a friend what a word means.

   D. increases prior knowledge, which facilitates comprehension.

2. Good questions enhance comprehension because they:

   A. free up attention from decoding.

   B. enhance prior knowledge.

   C. increase topic interest.

   D. provide purpose and structure for reading.

3. Question one above would be best classified as:

   A. text explicit.

   B. text implicit.

   C. experience-based.

   D. all of the above.

Performance Question

Explain why an automatic pilot for decoding is an important prerequisite for good reading comprehension.

Chapter 4 Self-Test

Matching

Match the definition with the appropriate term.

Terms

1. passage independent items

2. test validity

3. mirror assessment

4. testwiseness

5. passage dependent items

6. performance items

Definitions

A. The extent to which a test measures what it claims to measure.

B. Test questions that require written responses from students.

C. Test questions that can be answered without reading the passages to which they refer.

D. Classroom assessments that reflect the format of a standardized test.

E. A series of principles that can be applied to exams independently of subject-area knowledge.

F. Test questions that cannot be answered without reading the passages to which they refer.

Multiple-Choice Questions

Circle the letter of the best option.

1. Which of the following will result in the most valid test of reading ability?

   I. Passage dependent questions
  II. Passage independent questions
 III. Performance items
 IV. Vocabulary items

    A. I only

    B. I and II only

    C. II and IV only

    D. I, II, III, and IV

2. Which of the following testwiseness strategies is least likely to assist students on state reading assessments?

    A. Try to answer the questions before looking at the options.

    B. Never leave an answer blank.

    C. When in doubt, choose answer **C**.

    D. Eliminate obvious wrong answers.

    E. Review all of the options before choosing one.

3. Which of the following should not be a part of mirror assessment?

    A. Multiple-choice questions

    B. Open-book format

    C. Timed assessment

    D. One or more performance items

    E. Matching questions

Performance Question

Explain why subject-area teachers are better equipped than reading specialists to prepare most students for state reading assessments.

Answers to Chapter Self-Tests

Chapter 1: Rationale for Adolescent Literacy

Matching

    1. *C*   **2.** *A*   **3.** *B*

Multiple-Choice Questions

    1. *B*   **2.** *D*

Performance Question

Middle and secondary teachers emphasize the kind of reading instruction that focuses on aiding students in learning from print and online texts rather than on processes associated with beginning reading. Middle and secondary teachers encourage the thinking processes essential to understanding print and online text material (e.g., they act as facilitators for their students).

Chapter 2: Learning to Read

Matching

    1. *G*   **2.** *O*   **3.** *E*   **4.** *J*   **5.** *A*
    6. *D*   **7.** *K*   **8.** *B*   **9.** *L*   **10.** *M*
    11. *N*   **12.** *C*   **13.** *H*   **14.** *I*   **15.** *F*

Multiple-Choice Questions

    1. *B*   **2.** *A*   **3.** *B*

Performance Question

Words can only be recognized during fixations, which in adult fluent readers last about $\frac{1}{5}$ second. This leaves time for five fixations per second, with each fixation containing about two words. Without counting the time for saccades, regressions, and return sweeps, that would provide enough time to read about 10 words (five fixations × two words) per second and 600 words per minute (10 words per second × 60 seconds). This is the theoretical upper limit on reading speed and far less than claims of speed readers.

Chapter 3: Reading To Learn

Matching Questions

1. *G*   2. *A*   3. *B*   4. *E*   5. *C*   6. *D*   7. *F*

Multiple-Choice Questions

1. *D*   2. *D*   3. *B*

Performance Question

The autopilot eliminates the need for the reader to waste attention on decoding. This frees up attention for thinking during reading.

Chapter 4: Test Preparation Strategies

Matching

1. *C*   2. *A*   3. *D*   4. *E*   5. *F*   6. *B*

Multiple-Choice Questions

1. *A*   2. *C*   3. *E*

Performance Question

State reading assessments are also achievement tests because of their extensive use of passage independent questions and nonfiction texts from various subject areas. Prior knowledge of science, history, and other fields has a strong influence on student performance.

References Cited

Anders, P. L., and C. S. Bos. 1986. "Semantic feature analysis: An interactive strategy for vocabulary development and text comprehension." *Journal of Reading* 29: 610–616.

Baker, L. and L. C. Beall. 2009. "Metacognitive processes and reading comprehension." In *Handbook of research on reading comprehension*, Eds. S. E. Israel, and G. G. Duffy, 373-388. New York: Routledge.

Baldwin, R. S., J. E. Readence, and T.W. Bean. 2004. *Targeted reading: Improving achievement in middle and secondary grades.* Dubuque, IA: Kendall/Hunt.

Bean, T. W. 2010. *Multimodal learning for the 21st century adolescent.* Huntington Beach, CA: Shell Education.

Bean, T. W., and A. L. Bishop. 1992. "Polar opposites: A strategy for guiding students' critical reading and discussion." In *Reading in the content areas: Improving classroom instruction*, 3rd ed., Eds. E. K. Dishner, T. W. Bean, J. E. Readence, and D. W. Moore, 247–254. Dubuque, IA: Kendall/Hunt.

Bean, T. W. and H. Harper. 2011. "The context of English Language Arts learning: The high school years." In *Handbook of research on teaching the English Language Arts,* 3rd ed., Eds. D. Lapp and D. Fisher, 60–68. New York: Routledge.

Bean, T. W., J. E. Readence, and S. R. Baldwin. 2012. *Content area literacy: An integrated approach*, 10th ed. Dubuque, IA: Kendall/Hunt.

Biancarosa, G., and C. Snow. 2006. *Reading next: A vision for action and research in middle and high school literacy: A report to the Carnegie Corporation of New York*, 2nd ed. Washington, DC: Alliance for Excellent Education. Available: http://www.all4ed.org/publications/ReadingNext/ReadingNext.pdf.

Brum, G. D., P. Castro, and R. D. Quinn. 1978. *Biology and man.* Dubuque, IA: Kendall/Hunt.

Cartwright, K. B. 2009. "The role of cognitive flexibility in reading comprehension." In *Handbook of research on reading comprehension*, Eds. S. E. Israel, and G. G. Duffy, 115–139. New York: Routledge.

Conley, M. W., and K. A. Hinchman. 2004. "No child left behind: What it means for U.S. adolescents and what we can do about it." *Journal of Adolescent & Adult Literacy* 48 (1): 42–50.

Eanet, M., and A. V. Manzo. 1976. "REAP—A strategy for improving reading/writing/study skills." *Journal of Reading* 19: 647–652.

Grisham, J. 2003. *The King of Torts.* New York: Doubleday.

Heimlich, J. E., and S. D. Pittelman. 1986. *Semantic mapping: Classroom applications.* Newark, DE: International Reading Association.

Hopkins, G., and T. W. Bean. 1999. "Vocabulary learning with the verbal-visual word association strategy in a Native American community." *Journal of Adolescent & Adult Literacy* 42:274–281.

Kucan, L., and I. L. Beck. 1997. "Thinking aloud and reading comprehension research: Inquiry, instruction, and social interaction." *Review of Educational Research* 67:271–279.

Lee, C. D., and A. Spratley. 2010. *Reading in the disciplines: The challenges of adolescent literacy.* New York: Carnegie Corporation of New York. Available: http://carnegie.org/fileadmin/Media/Publications/PDF/tta_Lee.pdf.

Manzo, A., U. Manzo, and J. J. Albee. 2002. iREAP: "Improving reading, writing, and thinking in the wired classroom." *Journal of Adolescent & Adult Literacy* 46: 42–47.

McCauley, J. K., and D. S. McCauley. 1992. "Using choral reading to promote language learning for ESL students." *The Reading Teacher* 45: 526–533.

Moje, E. B. 2008. "Foregrounding the disciplines in secondary literacy teaching and learning: A call for change." *Journal of Adolescent & Adult Literacy* 52 (2): 96–107.

Ogle, D. M. 1986. "K-W-L: A teaching model that develops active reading of expository text." *The Reading Teacher* 39: 564–570.

Rasinski, T., N. Padak, R. M. Newton, and E. Newton. 2008. *Greek & Latin roots: Keys to building vocabulary*. Huntington Beach, CA: Shell Education.

Robinson, D. H. 1998. "Graphic organizers as aids to text learning." *Reading Research and Instruction* 37: 85–105.

Santa, C. M., S. C. Dailey, and M. Nelson. 1985. "Free-response and opinion-proof: A reading and writing strategy for middle grade and secondary teachers." *Journal of Reading* 28: 346–352.

Sartre, J. 1948. *The emotions: Outline of a theory*. New York: Book Sales.

Searfoss, L.W. 1975. "Radio reading." *The Reading Teacher* 29: 295–296.

Simpson, M. L., and S. L. Nist. 1990. The effects of PLAE upon students' test performance and metacognitive awareness. *Literacy theory and research: Analyses from multiple paradigms*. Thirty-ninth Yearbook of the National Reading Conference, Eds. J. Zutell and S. McCormick, 321-327. Chicago, IL: National Reading Conference.

Stahl, S. A., and B. A. Kapinus. 1991. "Possible sentences: Predicting word meanings to teach content area vocabulary." *The Reading Teacher* 45:36–43.

Tapscott, D. 2009. *Grown up digital: How the next generation is changing your world.* New York: McGraw Hill.

Vanderhoof, B. E., Miller, L. B. Clegg, and J. Patterson. 1992. "Real or fake? The phony document as a teaching strategy." *Social Education* 56:169–171.

Related Readings

Allington, R. J. 2002. "Research on reading/learning disability interventions." In *What research has to say about reading instruction*, 3rd ed., eds. A. E. Farstrup and S. J. Samuels, 261–290. Newark, DE: International Reading Association.

Armstrong, S. 2008. *Information literacy: Navigating & evaluating today's media*. Huntington Beach, CA: Shell Education.

Baumann, J. F., and M. F. Graves. 2010. "What is academic vocabulary?" *Journal of Adolescent & Adult Literacy* 54 (1): 4–12.

Bean, T. W. 2000. "Reading in the content areas: Social constructivist dimensions." In *Handbook of reading research: Volume III*, Eds. M. L. Kamil, P. B. Mosenthal, P. D. Pearson, and R. Barr, 629–644. Mahwah, NJ: Erlbaum.

———. 2002. "Making reading relevant for adolescents." *Educational Leadership* 60 (3): 34–37.

Bean, T. W., N. Walker, J. Wimmer, and B. Dillard. 2009. "How does creative content-area teaching work with adolescents?" In *Essential questions in adolescent literacy: Teachers and researchers describe what works in classrooms*, Ed. J. Lewis, 201–214. New York: The Guilford Press.

Blachowicz, C. L. Z., and P. Fisher. 2002. "Vocabulary instruction." In *Handbook of reading research: Volume III*, eds. M. L. Kamil, P. B. Mosenthal, P. D. Pearson, and R. Barr, 503–523. Mahwah, NJ: Erlbaum.

Brassell, D., and T. Rasinski. 2008. *Comprehension that works: Taking students beyond ordinary understanding to deep comprehension*. Huntington Beach, CA: Shell Education.

Buehl, D. 2001. *Classroom strategies for interactive learning*, 2nd ed. Newark, DE: International Reading Association.

Dillabough, D. 2008. *Text structures: Teaching patterns in reading and writing.* Toronto, ON: Thomson/Nelson.

Dishner, E. K., T. W. Bean, J. E. Readence, and D. W. Moore, eds. 1992. *Reading in the content areas: Improving classroom instruction*, 3rd ed. Dubuque, IA: Kendall/Hunt.

Farstrup, A. E., and S. J. Samuels. 2002. *What research has to say about reading instruction*, 3rd ed. Newark, DE: International Reading Association.

Gardiner, S. 2001. "Ten minutes a day for silent reading." *Educational Leadership* 59 (2):32–35.

Graves, M. F., and S. M. Watts-Taffe. 2002. The place of word consciousness in a research-based vocabulary program. In *What research has to say about reading instruction*, 3rd ed., Eds. A. E. Farstrup and S. J. Samuels, 140–165. Newark, DE: International Reading Association.

Kajder, S. B. 2006. *Bringing the outside in: Visual ways to engage reluctant readers.* Portland, ME: Stenhouse Publishers.

———. 2011. *Adolescents and digital literacies.* Urbana, IL: National Council of Teachers of English.

Macrorie, K. 1988. *The I-search paper.* Portsmouth, NH: Heinemann.

Moore, D. W., T. W. Bean, D. Birdyshaw, and J. A. Rycik. 1999. Adolescent literacy: A position statement. *Journal of Adolescent & Adult Literacy* 43:97–112.

Moore, D. W., and K. A. Hinchman. 2003. *Starting out: A guide to teaching adolescents who struggle with reading.* Boston: Allyn & Bacon.

Nagy, N. M., C. E. Campenni, and J. N. Shaw. 2000. A survey of sustained silent reading practices in seventh-grade classrooms. *Reading Online.* Available: http://www.readingonline.org/articles/nagy/ssr.html.

Nagy, W. E. and J. A. Scott. 2000. "Vocabulary processes." In *Handbook of reading research: Volume III*, Eds. M. L. Kamil, P. B. Mosenthal, P. D. Pearson, and R. Barr, 269–284. Mahwah, NJ: Erlbaum.

Nichols, M. 2008. *Talking about text: Guiding students to increase comprehension through purposeful talk.* Huntington Beach, CA: Shell Education.

Palmatier, R. A. 1971. "Comparison of four note-taking procedures." *Journal of Reading* 14:235–240.

Readence, J. E., R. S. Baldwin, and J. C. Ford. 1981. "Teaching word connotations: An alternative strategy." *Reading World* 21:103–108.

Readence, J. E., T. W. Bean, and R. S. Baldwin. 2001. *Content area literacy: An integrated approach*, 7th ed. Dubuque, IA: Kendall/Hunt.

Readence, J. E., D. W. Moore, and R. J. Rickelman. 2000. *Prereading activities for content area reading and learning*, 3rd ed. Newark, DE: International Reading Association.

Rillero, P., R. Zambo, J. Cleland, and J. Ryan. 1996. "Write from the start: Writing to learn science." *Science Scope* 19:30–32.

Scott, R. M. 2008. *Knowing words: Creating word-rich classrooms.* Toronto, ON: Thomson/Nelson.

Tierney, R. J., and J. E. Readence. 2005. *Reading strategies and practices: A compendium,* 6th ed. Boston, MA: Allyn & Bacon.

Tovani, C. 2000. *I read it, but I don't get it: Comprehension strategies for adolescent readers.* Portland, ME: Stenhouse Publishers.

Wood, K. D., and T. S. Dickinson. 2000. *Promoting literacy in grades 4–9: A handbook for teachers and administrators.* Boston: Allyn & Bacon.

Yopp, H. K., R. H. Yopp, and A. Bishop. 2009. *Vocabulary instruction for academic success.* Huntington Beach, CA: Shell Education.

Online Resources

A wealth of vocabulary, comprehension, and study resources are now available online to help your students' efforts to develop ownership of the material in your content area. These websites are not exhaustive, but they are helpful.

Academic Word List

Developed as an M.A. thesis at Victoria University of Wellington, New Zealand, the list contains 570 word families common to academic reading in the disciplines. Based on an analysis of their frequency, the list serves as a guide for students interested in mastering key technical and general vocabulary in the content areas. Available: http://www.nottingham.ac.uk/~alzsh3/acvocab/index.htm

Annenberg Classroom

This site offers lesson plans, videos, books, and other resources for middle and secondary school teachers. The Sunnyland Classroom provides examples of teachers and students using topical instructional resources, for example, activities related to the Constitution during the month of September. Available: http://www.annenbergclassroom.org

Annenberg Media Learner

This site provides a wealth of resources for language arts, history, literature, science, and other content areas. Resources include videos for high school students. Available: http://www.learner.org

Diigo

This research tool site offers students a Web 2.0 system for bookmarking, archiving, and annotating online information. Sticky notes can be added to bookmarked material, and annotated pages can be shared with others working on a project or presentation. Available: http://www.diigo.com

Inspiration

This site offers learners an array of graphic organizer tools to visually display information gleaned from reading print texts or online sources. Examples are provided for language arts, science, and social studies. Available: http://www.inspiration.com

International Reading Association

The organization's website offers a rich array of professional development resources in adolescent literacy. Use of some resources is limited to members of the organization. Available: http://www.reading.org

ReadWriteThink

ReadWriteThink is a rich resource for English and Language Arts teachers. Developed by two major literacy organizations, International Reading Association and the National Council of Teachers of English, this site features lesson and unit plans submitted and reviewed by educators for publication on the site. Major journals in the field (e.g. *Journal of Adolescent & Adult Literacy*) augment articles with URL links to this site. Available: http://www.readwritethink.org

RubiStar

This site offers templates you can use to construct your own four-point rubrics with ease. The templates eliminate headaches with formatting and include flexible categories and properties through pull-down menus. Available: http://rubistar.4teachers.org/index.php

Rubric Machine

This site has a wealth of prepared rubrics for many content areas. They can be adopted as is or used as models for your own classroom rubrics. Available: http://landmark-project.com/rubric_builder/index.php

Science NetLinks

This site features numerous lesson plans that support science standards. The plans include rich WebQuests and other resources useful in exploring topics like endangered species and others. Available: http://www.sciencenetlinks.com

Smithsonian Education

This Smithsonian Museum site features lesson plans that span science, history, literature, and other content areas. Available: http//www.smithsonianeducation.org

Thinkfinity

Sponsored by Verizon Foundation, *Thinkfinity* is the source of free lesson plans, interactive activities, and other online resources for K–12 teachers. The content is developed with the organization's partners, including the International Reading Association and National Council of Teachers of English (http://www.readwritethink.org); National Council of Teachers of Mathematics (http://illuminations.nctm.org); Council for Economic Education (http://www.econedlink.org); National Museum of American History (http://americanhistory.si.edu); and American Association for the Advancement of Science (http://www.sciencenetlinks.com). Available: http://www.thinkfinity.org

Vocabulary Lesson Plans

This site offers a collection of vocabulary sites to assist lesson and unit planning in several content areas, including English, science, math, geography, health, and social studies. Available: http://www.vocabulary-lesson-plans.com/vocabulary-websites.html